11th International Workshop on Natural Language Processing for Social Media (SocialNLP 2023)

Nusa Dua, Indonesia
1 November 2023

ISBN: 978-1-7138-9004-1

Printed from e-media with permission by:

Curran Associates, Inc.
57 Morehouse Lane
Red Hook, NY 12571

CURRAN ASSOCIATES INC.
proceedings.com

Some format issues inherent in the e-media version may also appear in this print version.

Association for Computational Linguistics
209 N. Eighth Street
Stroudsburg, Pennsylvania 18360

Phone: 1-570-476-8006
Fax: 1-570-476-0860

acl@aclweb.org

Additional copies of this publication are available from:

Curran Associates, Inc.
57 Morehouse Lane
Red Hook, NY 12571 USA
Phone: 845-758-0400
Fax: 845-758-2633
Email: curran@proceedings.com
Web: www.proceedings.com

IJCNLP-AACL 2023

The 11th International Workshop on Natural Language Processing for Social Media

Proceedings of the Workshop

November 1, 2023

The IJCNLP-AACL organizers gratefully acknowledge the support from the following sponsors.

Platinum

vivo

Gold

面壁智能
ModelBest

Silver

translated.

ZHIPU · AI

小牛翻译
NiuTrans.com

Message from the Organizers

It is our great pleasure to welcome you to the Eleventh Workshop on Natural Language Processing for Social Media-SocialNLP 2023, associated with IJCNLP-AACL 2023. SocialNLP is an inter-disciplinary area of natural language processing (NLP) and social computing. We hold SocialNLP twice a year: one in the NLP venue, the other in the associated venue such as those for web technology or artificial intelligence. This year the other version has been successfully held in conjunction with TheWebConf 2023, and we are very happily looking forward to the NLP version in IJCNLP-AACL 2023. We are very glad that the workshop is back to the fully in-person mode this year and we can meet our old and new friends. We keep high quality papers with the accepted threshold 3 (maximum 5), which again leads to a competitive selection process with the acceptance rate 55 percent. These exciting papers include various aspects and topics for researchers working on NLP for social media, such as food, drug and market research, humor and offensive language detection, sentiment and emotion analysis. We sincerely thank the authors for their contribution and believe they will benefit our research community.

This year we are excited to have Dr. David Adelani from University College London as our keynote speaker. He will talk about Social NLP for low-resource languages, which is especially vital now for creating an unbiased virtual social environment. We encourage attendees to attend our keynote speech as well as all our oral sessions to have more discussions with outstanding researchers.

Putting together SocialNLP 2023 was a team effort. We first thank the authors for providing the quality content of the program. We are grateful to the program committee members, who worked very hard in reviewing papers and providing feedback to authors. Finally, we especially thank the NAACL Workshop chairs Dr. Lun-Wei Ku and Prof. Kehai Chen for helping us on all the complicated logistics for this year's online version.

We hope you enjoy the workshop!

Organizers
Lun-Wei Ku, Academia Sincia, Taiwan
Cheng-Te Li, National Cheng Kung University, Taiwan

Organizing Committee

Lun-Wei Ku, Academia Sinica
Chenge-Te Li, National Cheng Kung University

Program Committee:

Liesbeth Allein, Katholieke Universiteit
Silvio Amir, Northeastern University
Yung-Chun Chang, Taipei Medical University
Huaping Zhang, Beijing Institute of Technology
Monojit Choudhury, Microsoft Research Lab India
Min-Yuh Day, National Taipei University
Yi-Li Hsu, Academia Sinica
Hen-Hsen Huang, National Chengchi University
Tsung-Ting Kuo, University of California San Diego
Chuan-Jie Lin, National Taiwan Ocean University
Manuel Montes, INAOE, Mexico
Derek Ruths, McGill University
Yohei Seki, University of Tsukuba
Boaz Shmueli, National Tsing Hua University and Institute of Information Science, Academia
Arpit Sood, Meta
Steven Wilson, The University of Edinburgh
Shih-Hung Wu, Chaoyang University of Technology
Liang-Chih Yu, Yuan Ze University
Zhe Zhang, IBM

Table of Contents

Conference Program

November 1

13:50–14:00 **Opening**
Chair: Lun-Wei Ku

14:00–14:50 *Keynote Speech: Social NLP for Low-resource Languages*
David Adelani, University College London, UK

14:50–15:30 **Sentiment and Emotion**

14:50–15:10 *Temporal Tides of Emotional Resonance: A Novel Approach to Identify Mental Health on Social Media*
Usman Naseem, Surendrabikram Thapa, Qi Zhang, Junaid Rashid, Liang Hu and Mehwish Nasim

15:10–15:30 *Efficient Sentiment Analysis: A Resource-Aware Evaluation of Feature Extraction Techniques, Ensembling, and Deep Learning Models*
Mahammed Kamruzzaman and Gene Kim

15:30–16:00 **Coffee Break**

16:00–17:20 **Aspects Related to Social Media**

16:00–16:20 *OffMix-3L: A Novel Code-Mixed Test Dataset in Bangla-English-Hindi for Offensive Language Identification*
Dhiman Goswami, Md Nishat Raihan, Antara Mahmud, Antonios Anastasopoulos and Marcos Zampieri

16:20–16:40 *An Emotion-Enriched and Psycholinguistics Features-Based Approach for Rumor Detection on Online Social Media*
Asimul Haque and Muhammad Abulaish

16:40–17:00 *The Future of Meat: Sentiment Analysis of Food Tweets*
Matiss Rikters and Maija Kāle

17:00–17:20 *Boosting Adverse Drug Event Normalization on Social Media: General-Purpose Model Initialization and Biomedical Semantic Text Similarity Benefit Zero-Shot Linking in Informal Contexts*
François Remy, Simone Scaboro and Beatrice Portelli

November 1 (continued)

17:20–17:30 Closing

Temporal Tides of Emotional Resonance: A Novel Approach to Identify Mental Health on Social Media

Usman Naseem[1], Surendrabikram Thapa[2], Qi Zhang[3,4], Junaid Rashid[5], Liang Hu[3,4], Mehwish Nasim[6,7]
[1]James Cook University, Australia [2]Virginia Tech, USA
[3]Tongji University, China [4]DeepBlue Academy of Sciences, China
[5]Sejong University, South Korea
[6]University of Western Australia [7]Flinders University, Australia

Abstract

Identifying mental health conditions using user-generated text on social media paved the way for automated computational methods for mental health surveillance on social media. Inferring the accurate state of mental health markers requires understanding the user's emotions and history of mental health conditions for identifying the mental health landscape of at-risk users. Existing works have exploited social media data by using users' most recent posts; however, previous works ignored users' emotional historical activity on social media, indicating their mental state over time. In this work, we address this gap and present a novel emotion- and time-aware architecture that jointly learns social media users' emotional historical context and temporal posting irregularities for mental health surveillance on social media. We conduct classification experiments to identify social media users with mental conditions, i.e., (i) healthy users and users affected with depression and (ii) healthy users and users prone to self-harm. Experimental results demonstrate proposed method outperforms recent competitive methods, demonstrating the importance of capturing the user's temporal emotional spectrum and time-aware emotional context through historical posts for social media users' mental health surveillance.

1 Introduction

According to the World Health Organization (WHO), one in four Americans has encountered mental conditions at some point in their lives (Consortium et al., 2004). About 4 – 8% of people in England will experience depression in their lifetime. Mental health has become a global concern and has procured more attention after the COVID-19 pandemic. Due to the high cost of mental health burden, computational research has even focused on analyzing mental health conditions using non-clinical data (Bucci et al., 2019; Moorhead et al.,

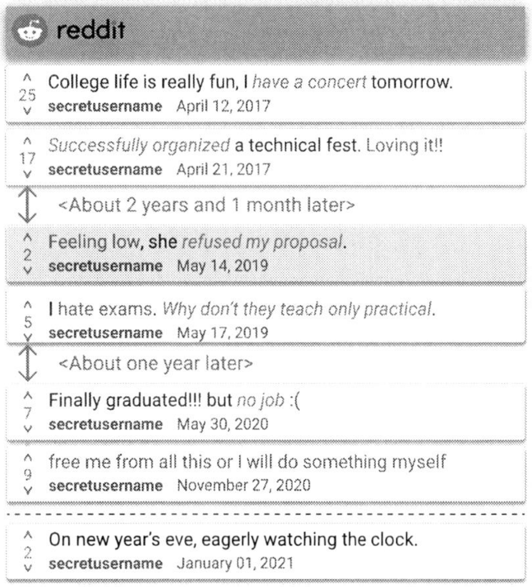

Figure 1: An example of a social media user with a mental health condition. Without analyzing the user's historical posts, which reflect depression inclinations, it is challenging to determine depression. Sequentially evaluating a user's postings without considering timing inconsistencies may misrepresent a user's mental state. Posts are paraphrased for ethical consideration.

2013; Adhikari et al., 2022; Thapa et al., 2020). Recent studies have shown that it is possible to learn about social media users' mental health conditions using user-generated text and behavioral analyses of their social media activity (Burke et al., 2010; Naseem et al., 2022a).

In particular, advancement in natural language processing (NLP) techniques and the availability of longitudinal data can play an essential role in assessing user-generated text on social media to identify risk markers for social media users (Naseem et al., 2022e,c). NLP methods can also help create a semi-automated system that can speed up the diagnosis process (Naseem et al., 2022d; Thapa et al., 2022; Adhikari et al., 2021). They may also

Proceedings of the 11th International Workshop on Natural Language Processing for Social Media, pages 1–8
November 1, 2023.

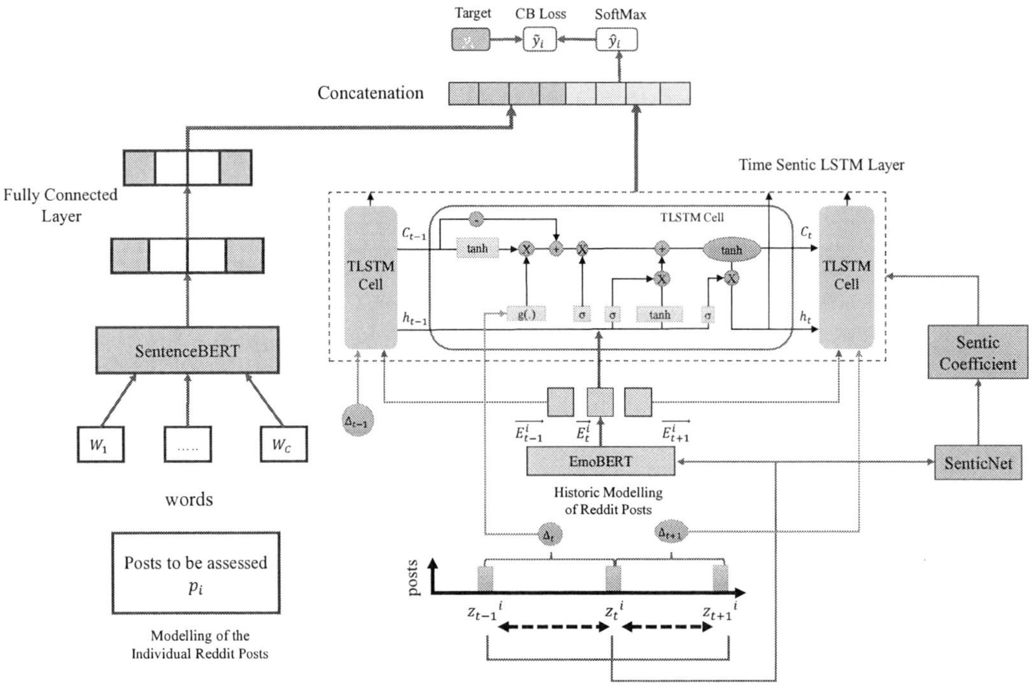

Figure 2: Overall architecture of proposed method

outperform traditional clinical prediction methods to detect mental health issues automatically by improving the specificity and speed of diagnosis (Ríssola et al., 2021). Furthermore, additional features, such as a user's social network (Zhou et al., 2015) or historical posts (Zogan et al., 2021; Naseem et al., 2023, 2022b), may also provide an auxiliary context in recognizing the development of negative emotions that are frequently associated with mental health conditions. Such data is likely to improve the performance of NLP models.

Relevant studies in this area focussed on context-aware sequential modeling (Tsakalidis et al., 2022; Ragheb et al., 2019), one-class-classification approach (Aguilera et al., 2021), time-aware LSTM models (Kang et al., 2022), emotion-based implicit lexicons (Aragón et al., 2019; Barros et al., 2021), and transformer-based classifiers (Martínez-Castaño et al., 2021; Maupomé et al., 2021). These NLP-based studies achieved desirable performance, albeit none of the studies leveraged user context for further performance improvement. We posit that studying users' historical, social media posts and emotion spectrum can help assess their risk of mental health conditions (Figure 1).

Researchers have captured user context as a bag-of-posts (Gaur et al., 2019) or sequentially (Cao et al., 2019; Matero et al., 2019; Zogan et al., 2021) for detecting social media users' mental health conditions. Though such methods are plausible, one of the major shortcomings is the inconsistent time interval between users' historical posts, which can have a critical impact on the correctness of the analysis. This implies that it is important to capture the gap between the user's current posts that are indicative of mental health conditions as well as those from previous years (Figure 1). Such temporal irregularities in users' historical posts affect users' evaluations. Sequential methods such as Long-Short-Term-Memory (LSTM) networks assume regular posting intervals, limiting the learning ability of a user's emotion spectrum over varied time intervals. In this study, we address these challenges. Our main contributions include the following:

- We present a novel architecture that jointly learns a user's emotional historical context and temporal posting irregularities for early detection of mental health issues on social media (section 2);
- We introduce Time-Sentic-LSTM, an extension of a time-aware LSTM, by incorporating components accounting for emo-

tional concept-level user's representation (section 2.2);

- Experimental results demonstrate that our method outperforms previous state-of-the-art methods for early detection of mental health issues using social media data (section 4).

2 Method

Overview of our architecture: The architecture of the proposed method is shown in Figure 2, which consists of the current post representation layer and the representation of the user's emotional historical spectrum, where we first encoded the individual historical posts and then modeled historical posts sequentially. In the subsequent discussion, we will explain each module in depth.

Problem Definition: We formally define the problem: given a social media user $u_i \in \{u_1, u_2, ..., u_n\}$ with historical posts $p_i \in \{p_1, p_2, ..., p_n\}$, *i* represents the number of posts. Our objective is early risk identification of the user with 1) depression and 2) self-harm risk using a user-level historical timeline. Each user post p_i is associated with history $Z_{i,j} = (z_1^i, \gamma_1^i), (z_2^i, \gamma_2^i), \cdots, (z_L^i, \gamma_L^i)$ where z_t^i is a historic post by the user u_j posted at time γ_k^i with $\gamma_1^i < \gamma_2^i <, \cdot, < \gamma_L^i < \gamma_{current}^i$. We formulate our problem as a binary classification task to predict a label y_i to the user u_i from the corresponding set of labels.

2.1 Current Post Representation

We used SentenceBERT (Reimers and Gurevych, 2019) to capture the linguistic features of a current post P_i. SentenceBERT calculates the mean of word output vectors to generate a fixed-size sentence embedding. This is formulated in eq. (1).

$$P_i = SentenceBERT(p_i) \tag{1}$$

where $P_i \in \mathbf{R}^{768}$ is transformed linearly using a dense layer with 768-dimensions.

2.2 User's Emotional Historic Spectrum

Individual historic post representation: Escalation in emotional aspects may represent an increased risk of depression and self-harm in Reddit posts. Hence, we extract the emotional spectrum of each historic post (z_k^i). General text encoders fail to capture fine-grained emotions from users' historical posts on social media. To mitigate that shortcoming, we capture fine-grained emotions using EmoBERT (Aduragba et al., 2021), a fine-tuned variant of BERT over fine-grained emotions of social media data associated with social well-being and reflected in implicit domain-specific emotions in posts.

Using EmoBERT, we tokenized each historical post and added the `[CLS]` token at the beginning of each post and used the final hidden state corresponding to the `[CLS]` token of 768-dimension as the aggregate representation of the emotional spectrum. We defined our emotional vector $(E_k^i) \in \mathbf{R}^{768}$ of each historic post z_k^i:

$$E_k^i = EmoBERT(z_k^i) \tag{2}$$

Emotional concept-level representation of user's historical posts: We introduced the use of SenticNet (Cambria et al., 2018) to extract the emotional concept-level representation of the user's historical posts and fuse it into the end-to-end training of an extension of an LSTM cell. To achieve this, a set of *C* concept candidates would be extracted using a syntactic concept parser and mapped to the d_c dimensional vectors $[\alpha_{t,1}, \alpha_{t,2}, ..., \alpha_{t,C}]$ at time step *t*. The candidate embedding of step *t* is calculated as the average of the vectors using eq 3:

$$\alpha_t = \frac{1}{C} \sum_i \alpha_{t,i} \tag{3}$$

Our extension of an LSTM cell is formulated as:

$$\begin{aligned}
f_t &= \sigma(W_f[x_t, h_{t-1}, \alpha_t] + b_f) \\
I_t &= \sigma(W_I[x_t, h_{t-1}, \alpha_t] + b_I) \\
\hat{C}_t &= \tanh(W_C[x_t, h_{t-1}] + b_c) \\
C_t &= f_t * C_{t-1} + I_t * \hat{C}_t \\
o_t &= \sigma(W_o[x_t, h_{t-1}, \alpha_t] + b_o \\
o_t^c &= \sigma(W_{co}[x_t, h_{t-1}, \alpha_t] + b_{co} \\
h_t &= 0_t * \tanh(C_t) + 0_t^c * \tanh(W_c\alpha_t)
\end{aligned}$$

where f_t, I_t, and o_t are the forget gate, input gate, and output gate, respectively. W_f, W_I, W_o, b_f, b_I and b_o are the weight matrix and bias scalar for each gate. C_t is the cell state, and h_t is the hidden output. The extracted emotional concepts are added to the forget, input, and output gates of an extended LSTM cell to capture sequential modeling of the user's historical posts.

Sequential historic post modeling: To capture the users' historical posts with irregular time intervals sequentially, we propose leveraging Time-aware LSTM (T-LSTM) (Baytas et al., 2017) where time lapse between posts is forwarded to the T-LSTM cell (Figure 2). The T-LSTM cell combines the actual time interval between posts, the emotional concept-level representation of the user's historical posts, and the emotional context of each historical post (E_k^i).

T-LSTM weights the short-term memory cell (C_t^S) and introduces memory time decay dependent on the time between consecutive posts. T-LSTM leverages a monotonically declining elapsed time mechanism to transform time into appropriate weights to achieve less impact on posts with larger elapsed time between posts. T-LSTM incorporates time lapses as follows:

$$C_{t-1}^S = \tanh(W_d C_{t-1} + b_d) \quad \text{(Short-term memory)}$$
$$\hat{C}_{t-1}^S = C_{t-1}^S * g(\Delta_t) \quad \text{(Discounted short-term memory)}$$
$$C_{t-1}^T = C_{t-1} + \hat{C}_{t-1}^S \quad \text{(Long-term memory)}$$
$$C_{t-1}^* = C_{t-1}^T + \hat{C}_{t-1}^S \quad \text{(Adjusted previous memory)}$$

where c_{t-1} and c_t are previous and current cell memories, and $\{W_d, b_d\}$ are model parameters. Δ_t is the time between user's historic posts i.e., z_{t-1} and z_t, $g(\Delta_t)$ is the decaying mechanism used in by Baytas et al. (2017). To derive the current hidden state ($\hat{H}_t^i$), T-LSTM changes LSTM gate operations by incorporating C_{t-1}^* in place of C_t.

2.3 Joint Network Optimization

The proposed method jointly learns the language of the current post and the user's emotional historic spectrum in a time-aware manner. To achieve this, we concatenate the encoded features of a current post (P_i) and $\hat{H}_t^i$ followed by a softmax function over a dense layer with Rectified Linear Unit (ReLU) to obtain the probability of the early risk detection. This is formulated as follows:

$$\begin{aligned} y_i &= RELU(W_y(P_i \oplus \hat{H}_t^i) + b_y) \\ \hat{y}_i &= softmax(y_i) \end{aligned} \tag{4}$$

where $\hat{y}_i$ is the final output and W_y, b_y are the model parameters.

To address the class imbalance, we trained our model using class balanced loss (Cui et al., 2019) along with focal loss (Lin et al., 2017). This loss method assigns class-wise re-weighting by incorporating an inversely proportionate weighting component and is defined as:

$$L = CB_{focal}(\hat{y}, y_i; \beta, \gamma) \tag{5}$$

where $\hat{y}_i$ is the predicted label, CB_{focal} is the class-balanced focal loss, and y_i is the label of the current tweet. β and γ are the hyperparameters.

3 Experimental Setup

3.1 Datasets

We evaluated the performance of our method on two datasets from CLEF eRISK[1] challenges: early risk detection of (i) self-harm and (ii) depression. We combined and used the data from the last three years in both datasets. The self-harm dataset includes 2,068 users labeled as *self-harm* (1,785) and *non-self-harm* (283). The depression dataset consists of 170 users labeled as *depressed* (16 users) and *non-depressed* (154 users). The statistics of the datasets we used are given in Table 1.

Stats\Datasets	Self-harm	Depression
No. of users	2,068	170
Class-wise distribution		
No self-harm/depression	44.58%	9.40%
self-harm/depression	19.53%	90.60%

Table 1: Datasets Statistics

3.2 Experimental Settings

For consistency, we used the same experimental settings for all models and used 10-fold cross-validation. All results are reported as the average across all folds. We used the grid search optimization technique to optimize the parameters. To tune the number of layers (n), we empirically experimented with the values: n $\in$ {1, 2, 3}. Similarly, for drop out (δ), we tested with: $\delta \in$ {0, 0.2, 0.4, 0.5, 0.8}, hidden dimension (H) with H $\in$ {64, 128, 256}, learning rate (lr): lr $\in$ {0.001, 0.005, 0.01, 0.02} and control parameter $\beta \in$ {0, 0.3, 0.6,....,3.0}. For optimization (O): O $\in$ {'Adam', 'Adamax', 'AdamaW'} with a batch size of 16 were used. We used base version pre-trained language models (LMs) using HuggingFace[2], an open-source Python library. Varying lengths of posts are padded and trained for 150 epochs with early stopping with a patience of 10 epochs. The hyper-parameters used in our experiments are n = 2, δ = 0.5, H = 128, O = AdamW, lr = 0.005, and β = 2. We will release our code publicly available for reproduction once the review is finished.

[1] https://erisk.irlab.org/
[2] https://huggingface.co/models

Baselines Methods\Datasets		Depression			Self Harm		
		Precision	Recall	F1-Score	Precision	Recall	F1-Score
Post-level	RF	0.45	0.50	0.47	0.44	0.50	0.47
	GRU	0.60	0.63	0.61	0.59	0.58	0.58
	LSTM	0.52	0.51	0.51	0.59	0.59	0.59
	C-LSTM	0.42	0.50	0.46	0.55	0.58	0.56
User-level	Contextual CNN	0.42	0.50	0.46	0.50	0.49	0.49
	Suicide Detection Model	0.46	0.47	0.46	0.57	0.58	0.57
	DualContextBert	0.56	0.63	0.59	0.62	0.56	0.59
	STATENet	0.57	0.56	0.56	0.56	0.54	0.55
	DepressionNet	0.61	0.63	0.62	0.61	0.59	0.60
	Our method	**0.72***	**0.67***	**0.69***	**0.63***	**0.62***	**0.62***

Table 2: Comparison of the proposed method v/s the baselines. F1, Precision, and Recall scores are averaged over 10 folds. * indicates that the proposed method achieved a significant ($p < 0.05$) performance improvement over the best baseline under Mann–Whitney U test.

3.3 Baselines

We validate the effectiveness of our model by comparing it with *post-level* and *user-level* baseline methods, which are widely used in previous similar studies.

- **Post-level baselines**

  Random Forest (RF): A non-contextual PL approach that applies random forest on their statistical and linguistic features (Sawhney et al., 2018b).

  Gated Recurrent Unit (GRU): We apply GRU model which undergo faster training of training data as compared to that of LSTM due to less number of parameters (Cho et al., 2014).

  Long-Short Term Memory (LSTM): We apply LSTM model for mapping emotional spectrum from historical timeline.

  Contextualized LSTM (C-LSTM): C-LSTM deep neural network uses CNN for feature extraction and LSTM for encoding posts (Sawhney et al., 2018a).

- **User-level baselines**

  Contextual CNN: A non-sequential UL model over posts encoded with GloVe embedding (Gaur et al., 2019).

  Suicide Detection Model: A user-level attention based LSTM model that encodes posts using FastText embedding (Cao et al., 2019).

  DualContextBERT: The best performing model at CLPsych 2019 which feeds BERT encoded posts to the attention-based RNN layer (Matero et al., 2019).

  STATENet: Suicidality assessment Time-Aware TEmporal Network, a transformer-based framework to identify suicidal risk on social media. STATENet uses a dual transformer-based architecture to learn tweets' linguistic and emotional cues (Sawhney et al., 2020).

  DepressionNet: A novel approach which summarizes user posts before encoding it via embedding. Authors apply the BiGRU model and concatenate the results with encoded current post (Zogan et al., 2021).

4 Results

4.1 Overall Comparison

Results in Table 2 explain the efficacy of our method as it outperforms the existing baselines on both datasets. The results with F1-Score are 0.69 and 0.62 for the depression and self-harm dataset, respectively, which is an absolute increase of 7% and 2%, respectively, compared to the DepressionNet. We observe better performance with the use of contextual features as compared to non-contextual feature-based methods. We attribute this to the reason that temporal context-based methods capture better insight into the mental state of users. Methods that sequentially capture the user's historical

Model	Depression	Self Harm
Current post only	0.54	0.56
Current + Sequential	0.59	0.59
Current + Time-aware	0.62	0.61
Our method	**0.69***	**0.62***

Table 3: Ablation analysis: F1-Scores are averaged over 10 folds. *indicates that the proposed method achieved a significant ($p < 0.05$) performance improvement over other variants under the Mann–Whitney U test.

post perform better than other methods, such as Context CNN. Recent advancement with DepressionNet recapitulates their ability to model temporal dependencies of historical posts compared to Context CNN's and DepressionNet. Our method performs better than other sequential-based baselines because it captures irregular time intervals in the posting history of a user using time-aware modeling, which enables our model to capture the user's emotional historical context accurately.

4.2 Ablation Study

We conduct an ablation study to evaluate the effectiveness of each component of our method (Table 3). The F1-Score drops on both datasets when we use only the current post of a user. The performance improves with sequential information followed by a time-aware model that captures irregular time intervals of users' historical postings and the user's emotional historic spectrum-based features. We conclude that the strengths of our method lie in the use of current post representation and the user's emotional historical spectrum.

5 Ethical Considerations

Our empirical work on the user's social media timeline does abide by ethical considerations. The metadata of self-reported writing on social media is sensitive and contains personal information and demographics. In this context, we incorporate the trade-off between privacy and the effectiveness of the proposed method. We present our work in a non-intrusive manner and do not specify any real-time examples in this research paper. We used the dataset available in the shared task of the eRISK workshop in the CLEF forum, studied it purely observationally, and did not intervene in the user's personal information. The annotated datasets we used are publicly available and include de-identified publicly available posts where users understand public access and there is no expectation of privacy. Hence, no ethical approval is required for this research.

6 Conclusion

We present a new emotion and time-aware architecture for social media users' mental health surveillance. Our method takes inspiration from psychological studies about analyzing a user's temporal emotional spectrum and capturing the time-aware emotional context of users through historical posts for more accurate mental health surveillance of social media users with self-harm and depression. The experimental results showed that our method outperformed previous methods for monitoring mental health conditions on social media.

Limitations

While our study presents a novel approach to mental health surveillance on social media, several limitations should be acknowledged. The reliance on user-generated text data assumes that individuals openly share their mental health experiences online, potentially introducing selection bias. Emotion detection from text data, while valuable, may not capture the full complexity of emotional states. The model's generalizability to diverse populations, platforms, and cultural contexts may require further validation. Interpretability and fairness in predictions, along with potential long-term impacts on individuals, deserve ongoing scrutiny.

References

Surabhi Adhikari, Surendrabikram Thapa, Usman Naseem, Priyanka Singh, Huan Huo, Gnana Bharathy, and Mukesh Prasad. 2022. Exploiting linguistic information from nepali transcripts for early detection of alzheimer's disease using natural language processing and machine learning techniques. *International Journal of Human-Computer Studies*, 160:102761.

Surabhi Adhikari, Surendrabikram Thapa, Priyanka Singh, Huan Huo, Gnana Bharathy, and Mukesh Prasad. 2021. A comparative study of machine learning and nlp techniques for uses of stop words by patients in diagnosis of alzheimer's disease. In *2021 International Joint Conference on Neural Networks (IJCNN)*, pages 1–8. IEEE.

Olanrewaju Tahir Aduragba, Jialin Yu, Alexandra I Cristea, and Lei Shi. 2021. Detecting fine-grained emotions on social media during major disease outbreaks: Health and well-being before and during the covid-19 pandemic. In *AMIA Annual Symposium Proceedings*, volume 2021, page 187. American Medical Informatics Association.

Juan Aguilera, Delia Irazú Hernández Farías, Manuel Montes-y Gómez, and Luis C González. 2021. Detecting traces of self-harm in social media: A simple and interpretable approach. In *Mexican International Conference on Artificial Intelligence*, pages 196–207. Springer.

Mario Ezra Aragón, Adrián Pastor López-Monroy, and Manuel Montes-y Gómez. 2019. Inaoe-cimat at erisk 2019: Detecting signs of anorexia using fine-grained emotions. In *CLEF (Working Notes)*.

Lucas Barros, Alina Trifan, and José Luís Oliveira. 2021. Vader meets bert: sentiment analysis for early detection of signs of self-harm through social mining. In *CLEF (Working Notes)*, pages 897–907.

Inci M Baytas, Cao Xiao, Xi Zhang, Fei Wang, Anil K Jain, and Jiayu Zhou. 2017. Patient subtyping via time-aware lstm networks. In *Proceedings of the 23rd ACM SIGKDD international conference on knowledge discovery and data mining*, pages 65–74.

Sandra Bucci, Matthias Schwannauer, and Natalie Berry. 2019. The digital revolution and its impact on mental health care. *Psychology and Psychotherapy: Theory, Research and Practice*, 92(2):277–297.

Moira Burke, Cameron Marlow, and Thomas Lento. 2010. Social network activity and social well-being. In *Proceedings of the SIGCHI conference on human factors in computing systems*, pages 1909–1912.

Erik Cambria, Soujanya Poria, Devamanyu Hazarika, and Kenneth Kwok. 2018. Senticnet 5: Discovering conceptual primitives for sentiment analysis by means of context embeddings. In *AAAI*.

Lei Cao, Huijun Zhang, Ling Feng, Zihan Wei, Xin Wang, Ningyun Li, and Xiaohao He. 2019. Latent suicide risk detection on microblog via suicide-oriented word embeddings and layered attention. In *Proceedings of the 2019 Conference on Empirical Methods in Natural Language Processing and the 9th International Joint Conference on Natural Language Processing (EMNLP-IJCNLP)*, pages 1718–1728.

Kyunghyun Cho, Bart Van Merriënboer, Dzmitry Bahdanau, and Yoshua Bengio. 2014. On the properties of neural machine translation: Encoder-decoder approaches. *arXiv preprint arXiv:1409.1259*.

WHO World Mental Health Survey Consortium et al. 2004. Prevalence, severity, and unmet need for treatment of mental disorders in the world health organization world mental health surveys. *Jama*, 291(21):2581–2590.

Yin Cui, Menglin Jia, Tsung-Yi Lin, Yang Song, and Serge Belongie. 2019. Class-balanced loss based on effective number of samples. In *Proceedings of the IEEE/CVF conference on computer vision and pattern recognition*, pages 9268–9277.

Manas Gaur, Amanuel Alambo, Joy Prakash Sain, Ugur Kursuncu, Krishnaprasad Thirunarayan, Ramakanth Kavuluru, Amit Sheth, Randy Welton, and Jyotishman Pathak. 2019. Knowledge-aware assessment of severity of suicide risk for early intervention. In *The World Wide Web Conference*, pages 514–525.

Xin Kang, Rongyu Dou, and Haitao Yu. 2022. Tua1 at erisk 2022: Exploring affective memories for early detection of depression.

Tsung-Yi Lin, Priya Goyal, Ross Girshick, Kaiming He, and Piotr Dollár. 2017. Focal loss for dense object detection. In *Proceedings of the IEEE international conference on computer vision*, pages 2980–2988.

Rodrigo Martínez-Castaño, Amal Htait, Leif Azzopardi, and Yashar Moshfeghi. 2021. Bert-based transformers for early detection of mental health illnesses. In *International Conference of the Cross-Language Evaluation Forum for European Languages*, pages 189–200. Springer.

Matthew Matero, Akash Idnani, Youngseo Son, Salvatore Giorgi, Huy Vu, Mohammad Zamani, Parth Limbachiya, Sharath Chandra Guntuku, and H Andrew Schwartz. 2019. Suicide risk assessment with multi-level dual-context language and bert. In *Proceedings of the Sixth Workshop on Computational Linguistics and Clinical Psychology*, pages 39–44.

Diego Maupomé, Maxime D Armstrong, Fanny Rancourt, Thomas Soulas, and Marie-Jean Meurs. 2021. Early detection of signs of pathological gambling, self-harm and depression through topic extraction and neural networks. In *CLEF (Working Notes)*, pages 1031–1045.

S Anne Moorhead, Diane E Hazlett, Laura Harrison, Jennifer K Carroll, Anthea Irwin, and Ciska Hoving. 2013. A new dimension of health care: systematic review of the uses, benefits, and limitations of social media for health communication. *Journal of medical Internet research*, 15(4):e1933.

Usman Naseem, Adam G Dunn, Jinman Kim, and Matloob Khushi. 2022a. Early identification of depression severity levels on reddit using ordinal classification. In *Proceedings of the ACM Web Conference 2022*, pages 2563–2572.

Usman Naseem, Matloob Khushi, Jinman Kim, and Adam G Dunn. 2022b. Hybrid text representation for explainable suicide risk identification on social media. *IEEE transactions on computational social systems*.

Usman Naseem, Jinman Kim, Matloob Khushi, and Adam Dunn. 2023. Graph-based hierarchical attention network for suicide risk detection on social media. In *Companion Proceedings of the ACM Web Conference 2023*, pages 995–1003.

Usman Naseem, Jinman Kim, Matloob Khushi, and Adam G Dunn. 2022c. Identification of disease or symptom terms in reddit to improve health mention classification. In *Proceedings of the ACM Web Conference 2022*, pages 2573–2581.

Usman Naseem, Jinman Kim, Matloob Khushi, and Adam G Dunn. 2022d. Robust identification of figurative language in personal health mentions on twitter. *IEEE Transactions on Artificial Intelligence*, 4(2):362–372.

Usman Naseem, Byoung Chan Lee, Matloob Khushi, Jinman Kim, and Adam G Dunn. 2022e. Benchmarking for public health surveillance tasks on social media with a domain-specific pretrained language model. *NLP-Power 2022*, page 22.

Waleed Ragheb, Jérôme Azé, Sandra Bringay, and Maximilien Servajean. 2019. Attentive multi-stage learning for early risk detection of signs of anorexia and self-harm on social media. In *CLEF 2019 Working Notes-Conference and Labs of the Evaluation Forum*, volume 2380, page 126.

Nils Reimers and Iryna Gurevych. 2019. Sentence-bert: Sentence embeddings using siamese bert-networks. *arXiv preprint arXiv:1908.10084*.

Esteban A Ríssola, David E Losada, and Fabio Crestani. 2021. A survey of computational methods for online mental state assessment on social media. *ACM Transactions on Computing for Healthcare*, 2(2):1–31.

Ramit Sawhney, Harshit Joshi, Saumya Gandhi, and Rajiv Shah. 2020. A time-aware transformer based model for suicide ideation detection on social media. In *Proceedings of the 2020 conference on empirical methods in natural language processing (EMNLP)*, pages 7685–7697.

Ramit Sawhney, Prachi Manchanda, Puneet Mathur, Rajiv Shah, and Raj Singh. 2018a. Exploring and learning suicidal ideation connotations on social media with deep learning. In *Proceedings of the 9th Workshop on Computational Approaches to Subjectivity, Sentiment and Social Media Analysis*, pages 167–175.

Ramit Sawhney, Prachi Manchanda, Raj Singh, and Swati Aggarwal. 2018b. A computational approach to feature extraction for identification of suicidal ideation in tweets. In *Proceedings of ACL 2018, Student Research Workshop*, pages 91–98.

Surendrabikram Thapa, Surabhi Adhikari, Usman Naseem, Priyanka Singh, Gnana Bharathy, and Mukesh Prasad. 2020. Detecting alzheimer's disease by exploiting linguistic information from nepali transcript. In *Neural Information Processing: 27th International Conference, ICONIP 2020, Bangkok, Thailand, November 18–22, 2020, Proceedings, Part IV 27*, pages 176–184. Springer.

Surendrabikram Thapa, Awishkar Ghimire, Surabhi Adhikari, Akash Kumar Bhoi, and Paolo Barsocchi. 2022. Cognitive internet of things (iot) and computational intelligence for mental well-being. In *Cognitive and Soft Computing Techniques for the Analysis of Healthcare Data*, pages 59–77. Elsevier.

Adam Tsakalidis, Federico Nanni, Anthony Hills, Jenny Chim, Jiayu Song, and Maria Liakata. 2022. Identifying moments of change from longitudinal user text. *arXiv preprint arXiv:2205.05593*.

Xujuan Zhou, Enrico Coiera, Guy Tsafnat, Diana Arachi, Mei-Sing Ong, Adam G Dunn, et al. 2015. Using social connection information to improve opinion mining: Identifying negative sentiment about hpv vaccines on twitter.

Hamad Zogan, Imran Razzak, Shoaib Jameel, and Guandong Xu. 2021. Depressionnet: A novel summarization boosted deep framework for depression detection on social media. *arXiv preprint arXiv:2105.10878*.

Efficient Sentiment Analysis: A Resource-Aware Evaluation of Feature Extraction Techniques, Ensembling, and Deep Learning Models

Mahammed Kamruzzaman
University of South Florida
Tampa, FL, USA 33620
kamruzzaman1@usf.edu

Gene Louis Kim
University of South Florida
Tampa, FL, USA 33620
genekim@usf.edu

Abstract

Huge amounts of sentiment-rich data are produced on social networks, the rate of which is growing year by year. As such, a global view of sentiment on social media platforms is only possible at scale through automation. The huge data sizes also mean that sentiment analysis systems must balance both accuracy and computing resource requirements. Typical NLP research maximizes accuracy, while other metrics are overlooked and thus older models are forgotten. Prior models are easily forgotten despite their possible suitability in settings where large computing resources are unavailable or relatively more costly. In this paper, we perform a broad comparative evaluation of document-level sentiment analysis models with a focus on resource costs that are important for the feasibility of model deployment and general climate consciousness. Our experiments consider different feature extraction techniques, the effect of ensembling, task-specific deep learning modeling, and domain-independent large language models (LLMs). We find that while a fine-tuned LLM achieves the best accuracy, some alternate configurations provide huge (up to $24,283\times$) resource savings for a marginal (<1%) loss in accuracy. Furthermore, we find that for smaller datasets, the differences in accuracy shrink while the difference in resource consumption grows further. [1]

1 Introduction

The wider NLP community in recent years has seen a trend in growing models and data sizes to improve performance. This trend is most clearly demonstrated by the progression of large language models over the past few years, from ELMo (Peters et al., 2018), followed by BERT (Devlin et al., 2019), RoBERTa (Liu et al., 2019), GPT-3 (Brown et al., 2020), and LaMDA (Thoppilan et al., 2022), just to name several notable examples, though this is by no means the only area of NLP where this is happening. This trend leaves resource efficiency and sustainability as an afterthought, a luxury that social media platforms may not have due to the sheer amount of data produced on social networks. Resource-intensive models not only cost more but also have a greater carbon impact—a consideration that is increasingly important to make in a climate-conscious society.

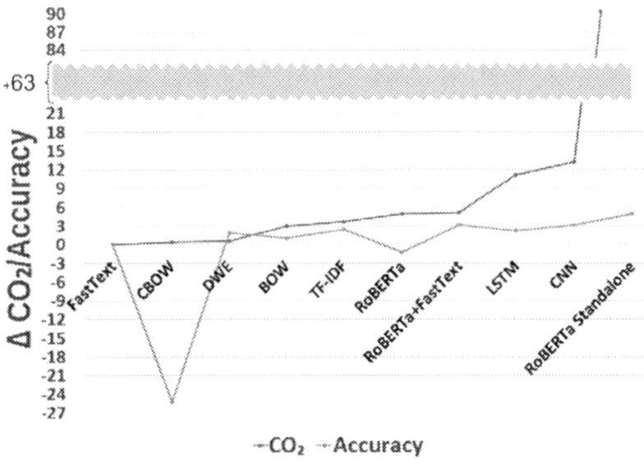

Figure 1: Change in accuracy and estimated grams of CO_2 emitted from various feature extraction models and the standalone fine-tuned RoBERTa model on the IMDB dataset (Maas et al., 2011). Plotted values are averages across all considered classifiers. The changes in values (ΔCO_2 / accuracy) were computed relative to FastText, which had the lowest CO_2 of all feature extractors we considered. For full results see Table 1.

Ensemble methods are another common, though more old-fashioned, technique for attaining performance improvements. Ensemble learning combines the results of several models and frequently achieves state-of-the-art (SOTA) results in benchmarks across NLP domains. These models are often only outperformed by large language models that have been pretrained on vast amounts of data. Notable examples in NLP include the Graphene algorithm for AMR Parsing (Hoang et al., 2021),

[1]The source code for our evaluations is available at https://github.com/kamruzzaman15/Sentiment-Analysis-Feature-Extraction-.

Proceedings of the 11th International Workshop on Natural Language Processing for Social Media, pages 9–20
November 1, 2023. ©2023 Association for Computational Linguistics

the SQuAD 2.0 question answering task (Rajpurkar et al., 2018) where ensemble models consistently beat single-models of comparable complexity. In these performance-topping scenarios, the ensemble learning methods lead to increased computing costs and associated greenhouse gas emissions due to the multiple models that make up the ensemble.

In this paper, we investigate the relationships between system performance, computing costs, and environmental costs while considering both large pretrained models and ensembling methods to find an accurate view of the trade-offs that we make when we select one model over another. Performance analysis in the literature often limits its view to only measuring the quality of the output (e.g., accuracy), ignoring both real-world resource constraints such as time and memory requirements and the relative environmental impact of using one model over another.

We use the task of document-level sentiment analysis as a case study. This ensures that the experiments stay within the scope of a single paper and that we avoid an explosion of experimental settings. Social networks produce huge amounts of sentiment-rich data in various forms, such as comments, reviews, and customer service chat, which are difficult to parse manually. Sentiment analysis is a critical tool for providing a global view of sentiment on a social media platform.

In our investigation, we use three different review datasets and consider nine feature extraction methods, two ensembling methods, and three standalone models. The wide range of datasets and methods ensures we can identify broad trends and make replicable conclusions.

This paper's contributions are the following.

- We investigate the relationship between performance, resource use, and environmental impact in sentiment analysis by measuring accuracy, end-to-end runtime, memory usage, energy expenditure, and generated CO_2 estimates for a broad range of models that previous literature has shown to be appropriate for this task.

- We find that although modern neural systems can outperform other methods in accuracy, this comes at a considerable cost in other resources (time, memory, and energy). The performance advantage of large neural models over other methods shrinks on smaller datasets, making alternatives more appealing.

- For most of the scenarios that we tested, we find that FastText with a Support Vector Machine (SVM) classifier or a frozen RoBERTa model (no finetuning) alongside FastText and an SVM classifier achieves strong performance while greatly reducing runtime and energy expenditure.

Figure 1 demonstrates all three points for feature extractors on the IMDB review dataset. It shows how accuracy and carbon emissions change across feature extractors, including the extreme carbon emissions cost of the fine-tuned RoBERTa model and the balanced accuracy and emissions of the RoBERTa+FastText feature extractor.

2 Related Work

Strubell et al. (2019) revealed that recent NLP advancements have come with significant financial, energy, and environmental costs. Hershcovich et al. (2022) suggest that addressing this issue requires an emphasis in promoting climate transparency in research. In this vein, Pranesh and Shekhar's (2020) analysis clearly reveals resource efficiency differences in several text classification models. Their analysis, however, did not include now-prevalent LLMs and only considered memory efficiency. Bannour et al. (2021) brought CO_2 measurement into such model comparison and recommended ML CO2 (Lacoste et al., 2019) as a convenient carbon tracking tool. ML CO_2 has since developed into codecarbon (Lottick et al., 2019), which we use for our experiments.

Previous studies in sentiment analysis have investigated a wide range of methodologies, including traditional machine learning models, deep machine learning models, and various feature extraction strategies. Dataset-based feature extraction techniques such as bag-of-words (BOW), TF-IDF, and n-grams had historically been popular in sentiment analysis. Similarly, FastText, GloVe, and word2vec were popular pretrained word embeddings in sentiment analysis and other NLP classifications alike. Zhou et al. (2022) proposed a model that uses the double word embedding (DWE) method for sentiment classification, where GloVe and word2vec are used in combination for input. Alharbi et al. (2021) and Goularas and Kamis (2019) focused on pretrained word embedding models with neural networks. Alharbi et al. (2021) compared GloVe, word2vec, and FastText word embedding models with various RNN architectures. Goularas and

Kamis (2019) considered GloVe and word2vec embeddings with multiple CNN and RNN architectures. They proposed a method of combining multiple CNNs with a biLSTM using GloVe embeddings as input, which they showed to outperform the other configurations in terms of accuracy.

3 Methodology

We separate our models into two broad categories. One category contains models based on an arbitrary combination of a feature extractor and a classifier. The other category contains standalone models where at least one of these two components is inherent to the model design. The input for all models is preprocessed in the same manner and all models are trained to produce a binary sentiment polarity classification. Figure 2 illustrates the high-level data flow from the review dataset to the output for the two types of models. For data preprocessing details see Appendix A. See Appendix B for a discussion of feature extractors, classifiers, and standalone models that were abandoned from our final evaluation. The remainder of this section provides brief introductions to each of the feature extractors, classifiers, and standalone models that we consider in our experiments.

3.1 Feature Extraction Methods

Bag of Words (BOW). BOW is a classic, simple approach to converting text data into a vector that can be input into an ML model. Each document is represented by a V dimensional vector, where V is the vocabulary size. Each dimension value corresponds to the number of times the word appears in the text.

Term Frequency-Inverse Document Frequency (TF-IDF). TF-IDF combines the term frequency and inverse document frequency to produce a value representing the relevance of a word to a document (Salton and Buckley, 1988). The term frequency is the number of times the word appears in the text. The inverse document frequency is the inverse of the number of documents that the word appears in. This ensures that words that are common across texts, such as function words, are not over-valued. TF-IDF unfortunately may become computationally expensive for large vocabularies.

Continuous Bag of Words (CBOW). The CBOW model encodes the meaning of words using the several surrounding context words as feedback (Mikolov et al., 2013). From this, it predicts contextually correct sentences. As CBOW models are able to make use of more data during the input than the Skip-gram model (Mikolov et al., 2013), they can capture the word vectors efficiently and hence perform better than Skip-gram. We trained our CBOW model using the word2vec module in the Gensim library (Řehůřek and Sojka, 2010).

FastText. FastText (Bojanowski et al., 2016; Joulin et al., 2017) is a highly engineered library by Facebook for representation learning and classification exploiting subword information and quantization-based memory optimizations. We use a supervised learning algorithm to train FastText on our specific training data, which allows us to learn word embeddings from each dataset. Further details of this system are beyond the scope of this paper.

Double Word Embedding (DWE). DWEs were introduced by Zhou et al. (2022) as a method to obtain combine the benefits of two different word embedding schemes using a convolution layer with piece-wise max pooling. We use DWEs combining FastText and GloVe whereas Zhou et al. (2022) used GloVe and word2vec based on preliminary experiments on all combinations of the three word embedding models. Word-level GloVe vectors are mean-pooled to obtain document-level vectors. FastText vectors are obtained according to the same approach as described in the FastText section.

CNN. Our convolutional neural network (CNN) feature extractor has the following architecture, which is described below. Each convolution layer is followed by ReLU activation, max pooling, and dropout. For training, after the final convolution layer (+ aforementioned post-convolution steps) the data is fed through two dense layers and a sigmoid. When used as a feature extractor, the feature embeddings are pulled from the last convolution layer, before the max pooling stage, but after ReLU activation. These are fed into the classifiers. For the IMDB dataset, we use two convolution layers. For the smaller restaurant and product review datasets, we only use a single convolution layer.

LSTM. Long short-term memory networks (LSTMs) are designed to learn long-term dependencies in the input, such as those seen in text data. Our LSTM design is similar to our CNN feature extractor. Each LSTM layer is followed

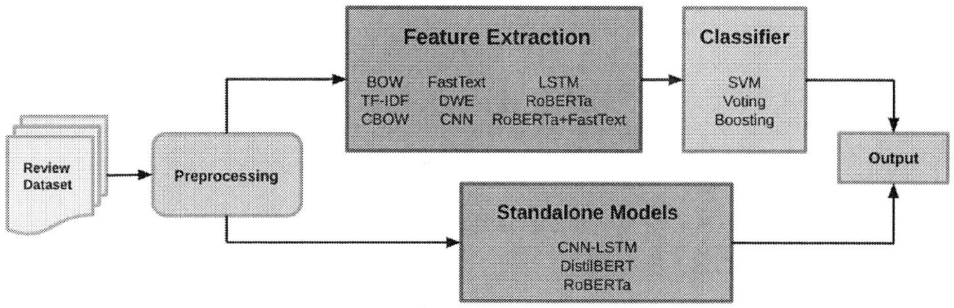

Figure 2: High-level data flow from the review dataset to the output for models composed of feature extractors with classifiers and standalone models.

by a dropout layer. During training, prediction is done after two additional dense layers and a sigmoid activation. When used as a feature extractor, features are pulled from the last LSTM layer before dropout and fed into classifiers. We use two LSTM layers for the IMDB dataset and one layer for the two smaller datasets.

RoBERTa. We use the 12th hidden layer for the [CLS] token of the RoBERTa-base model as the feature vector. When used as a feature extractor, RoBERTa is fully frozen and never trained.

RoBERTa + FastText. FastText and RoBERTa feature vectors—as described in FastText and RoBERTa section above—are concatenated to create a joint representation of the input text data.

3.2 Classification Models

SVM. Support vector machines (SVMs) select the hyperplane that divides the data points into labeled classes while maintaining a margin between the hyperplane and the nearest data point(s) (Hearst et al., 1998). For binary classification, this hyperplane is positioned to accomplish the maximum separation between the two classes, resulting in the largest possible margin. SVMs are popular classifiers, especially in machine learning application domains, due to their robustness to small dataset sizes.

Voting Ensemble. Voting ensembles take the predictions ("votes") from member classifiers and select the winning vote. We use a soft-voting method described by Witten et al. (2011), where each member classifier produces a probability distribution over the possible classes, and the class with the highest average probability wins. We use SVM, Random Forest (RF), and Multinomial Naïve Bayes (MNB) as the member classifiers in our experiments.

Boosting Ensemble. Boosting is a sequential ensemble process for changing the weight of observations based on the previous classifications iteratively. When an observation is wrongly labeled, the weight of the observation rises. This eliminates dataset bias error and generates robust statistical models. During preparation, the Boosting algorithm assigns weights to each of the resulting models. For boosting, we use XGBoost (eXtreme Gradient Boosting) (Chen and Guestrin, 2016).

3.3 Standalone Models

In initial experiments, we found that changing the classification head led to a consistent decrease in performance for certain neural models. This suggests that the feature extraction stages of these models are interwoven with the classification method over which they are trained. In these cases, we keep both the feature extraction and classification components together without swapping out classification heads.

CNN-LSTM. Following Goularas and Kamis (2019), we use a combination of CNN and LSTM to extract the local and global characteristics in the input text. Each CNN layer is followed by ReLU activation, max pooling, and dropout. The first CNN layer takes randomly initialized vocabulary vectors as input. The LSTM layers then run on top of this. Each LSTM layer is followed by dropout. Finally, two dense layers and a sigmoid activation are used for prediction. For the IMDB dataset, we use two CNN and LSTM layers each. For the restaurant and product review datasets, we only use a single layer each.

IMDB Review Dataset						
Feature Extraction Method	Classifier	Accuracy	Time (min)	Memory (MB)	Energy (Wh)	CO_2(g.)
BOW	SVM	87.86	18.75	178.72	3.66	1.701
	Voting	88.06	82.01	181.61	16.02	7.442
	Boosting	85.40	0.16	152.82	0.03	0.015
TF-IDF	SVM	90.11	22.87	179.36	4.46	2.075
	Voting	89.82	103.93	182.28	20.30	9.432
	Boosting	85.56	0.22	154.21	0.04	0.020
CBOW	SVM	61.43	3.60	106.41	0.70	0.327
	Voting	61.26	10.29	106.36	2.011	0.934
	Boosting	60.10	2.12	79.07	0.41	0.192
FastText	SVM	88.64	0.34	65.58	0.06	0.031
	Voting	81.25	2.38	66.06	0.46	0.216
	Boosting	88.40	**0.08**	**60.69**	**0.01**	**0.007**
DWE	SVM	88.72	5.24	745.46	1.02	0.476
	Voting	86.47	11.22	732.16	2.19	1.018
	Boosting	88.73	3.25	710.59	0.63	0.295
CNN	SVM	89.59	89.82	6519.82	17.54	8.151
	Voting	89.65	337.81	6519.87	65.98	30.655
	Boosting	88.63	11.16	5150.24	2.81	1.013
LSTM	SVM	88.62	123.10	361.67	24.04	11.172
	Voting	88.37	126.95	362.14	24.80	11.521
	Boosting	87.87	122.45	355.43	23.92	11.112
RoBERTa	SVM	83.88	54.59	774.55	10.66	4.953
	Voting	85.78	68.07	732.08	13.29	6.176
	Boosting	84.60	43.42	632.45	8.48	3.941
RoBERTa + FastText	SVM	89.51	57.47	789.90	11.22	5.214
	Voting	89.27	69.01	747.43	13.45	6.250
	Boosting	88.94	44.80	691.29	8.75	4.065
Standalone RoBERTa Baseline		**91.02**	997.88	606.14	201.05	90.554

Table 1: Results of IMDB review dataset on various combinations of feature extraction methods and classifiers.

RoBERTa-base. When used as a standalone model, we jointly fine-tune all layers of the RoBERTa base model and train the classifier on each dataset. We obtain a RoBERTa base model classifier using the Huggingface (Wolf et al., 2020) AutoModel feature for sequence classification.

DistilBERT-base-uncased. We use DistilBERT base uncased model as a standalone model in our experiment. This model is fine-tuned with an added classification layer in the same manner as the RoBERTa base model.

4 Experimental Setup

All experiments were conducted on a single workstation in Florida, USA. For more details of the workstation configuration see Appendix C.

Datasets. We evaluate our models on three different binary sentiment classification datasets. We evaluate our model configurations on the IMDB movie review dataset (Maas et al., 2011), the "Restaurant Reviews in Dhaka, Bangladesh" dataset (Adhikary, 2019), and the "Grammar and Online Product Review" dataset (Datafiniti, 2018). Following Zhang et al. (2015) and Agarwal et al. (2011), we construct a binary classification task from restaurant and product review datasets by labeling 1-star samples as negative polarity and 5-star samples as positive polarity examples. For more details of datasets see Appendix D. In all of our experiments, 80% of the data is used for training and 20% for testing.

Model Parameters. The context window size of the CBOW model is set to 15 and the min-count is set to 1 so that it considers all words. For SVM, MNB, and RF, we use the default parameters provided by the `scikit-learn` library (Pedregosa et al., 2011). For the XGBoost classifier, we use the default parameters of the `xgboost` library (Chen and Guestrin, 2016). We adjust the non-pretrained neural models based on different sizes of the datasets. For more details about these parameters see Appendix E.

Training Parameters. For the CNN-LSTM models, we choose the number of epochs between 2 and 5 depending on the dataset size. For the restaurant and product review dataset, the batch size is 32 and for IMDB, the batch size is 16. Adaptive Moment Estimation is used as an optimizer with binary

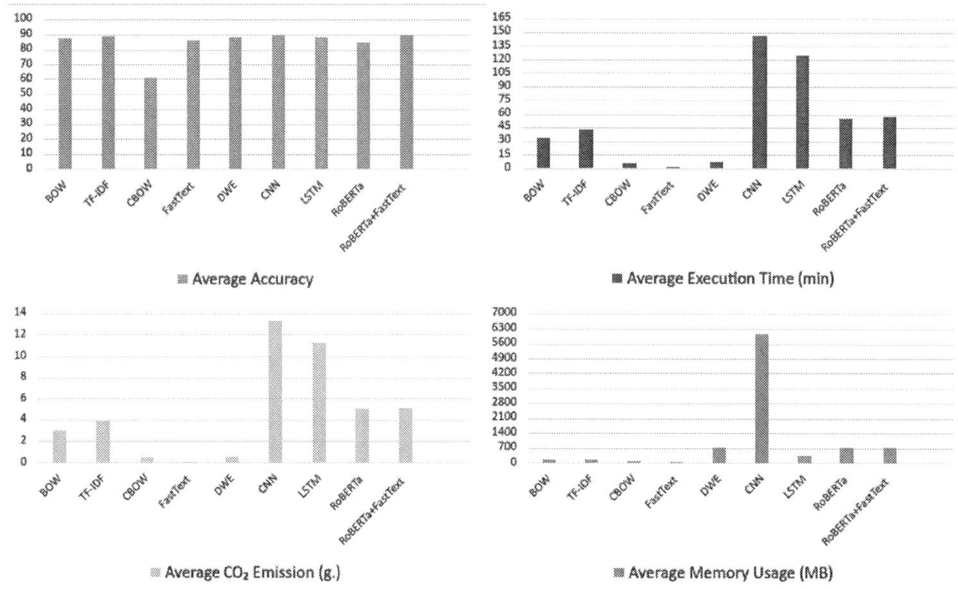

Figure 3: Feature extraction results for the IMDB dataset, averaged across classifiers.

cross-entropy loss. The CNN and LSTM feature extractors are only trained for 1 epoch each. The fine-tuned RoBERTa-base model is trained with a learning rate of 1e-1, accumulation steps of 2, and batch size of 8. We train it for 3 epochs using the AdamW optimizer. DistilBERT is trained with a batch size of 16. Otherwise, the parameters are the same as RoBERTa.

Evaluation Metric. To evaluate our models we measure accuracy, end-to-end execution time or total time, and memory measurement that includes the memory usage of both the model itself (model size) and the memory consumed during the forward pass or inference, electricity consumption, and CO_2 emissions. We use codecarbon (Lottick et al., 2019) to estimate the carbon emissions.

5 Results & Analysis

The full results on the IMDB, restaurant, and product review datasets for various feature extraction-classifier combinations are provided in Table 1, Table 2, and Table 3, respectively, alongside the standalone RoBERTa model. In every table, CO_2 emissions are measured in grams, energy consumption in Watt-hours (Wh), time in minutes, and memory in megabytes (MB). Figure 3 plots the average accuracy, CO_2, time, and memory usage for each feature extraction technique on the IMDB dataset. The same plot for the restaurant review dataset (Figure 4) is provided in Appendix F. Looking at only the accuracy numbers, we find that the fine-tuned RoBERTa model outperforms every other configuration in every dataset. However, upon closer inspection, we find that the story is not so simple.

Feature Extractors and Classifiers. In Table 1, we see that the standalone RoBERTa model achieves the best accuracy of 91.02%, followed by TF-IDF, FastText, and RoBERTa + FastText feature extractors with the SVM classifier, which achieve 90.11%, 88.64%, and 89.51%, respectively. If we take a look at the carbon emissions, these models do considerably better than the standalone RoBERTa model. TF-IDF with SVM results in 43 times less carbon emissions with only a 0.91% accuracy reduction. Similarly, RoBERTa + FastText with SVM produces 17 times less carbon emissions, while DWE with boosting produces 306 times less carbon emission, resulting in 1.51% and 2.29% accuracy reductions, respectively. When taking these other resources into consideration, FastText may be a better option than the fine-tuned RoBERTa model. The CNN feature extractor achieved competitive accuracy but has considerable memory requirements. It is also worth mentioning that end-to-end runtime and CO_2 for CNN as a feature extractor with SVM and Voting is more than the RoBERTa as a feature extractor because the feature layer of CNN is computationally intensive for its number of filters and kernels.

Table 2 shows similar results for the restaurant

Restaurant Review Dataset						
Feature Extraction Method	Classifier	Accuracy	Time (min)	Memory (MB)	Energy (Wh)	CO_2 (g.)
BOW	SVM	94.51	0.041	6.74	0.008	0.0037
	Voting	95.76	0.233	7.24	0.046	0.0211
	Boosting	94.80	0.008	**6.10**	0.002	0.0007
TF-IDF	SVM	95.62	0.045	6.90	0.009	0.0040
	Voting	95.81	0.248	7.39	0.048	0.0225
	Boosting	94.56	0.008	6.29	0.002	0.0007
CBOW	SVM	77.88	0.078	12.69	0.015	0.0071
	Voting	78.75	0.347	12.92	0.068	0.0315
	Boosting	80.33	0.052	10.04	0.012	0.0054
FastText	SVM	96.01	**0.007**	6.41	**0.001**	**0.0006**
	Voting	92.11	0.101	6.77	0.020	0.0092
	Boosting	95.91	0.011	6.18	0.002	0.0010
DWE	SVM	96.10	2.055	553.84	0.402	0.1866
	Voting	93.79	2.259	552.60	0.442	0.2051
	Boosting	95.86	2.008	550.33	0.393	0.1824
CNN	SVM	96.05	4.029	3044.51	0.787	0.3655
	Voting	95.62	16.168	3044.75	3.157	1.4666
	Boosting	95.28	2.751	2641.68	0.537	0.2496
LSTM	SVM	94.85	5.652	62.40	1.104	0.5129
	Voting	95.14	6.161	62.63	1.204	0.5591
	Boosting	95.24	5.608	62.06	1.096	0.5089
RoBERTa	SVM	80.24	5.133	149.62	1.003	0.4657
	Voting	92.12	5.826	142.68	1.138	0.5286
	Boosting	93.84	4.902	130.15	0.957	0.4447
RoBERTa + FastText	SVM	96.53	5.921	151.01	1.156	0.5372
	Voting	96.25	6.129	150.92	1.197	0.5561
	Boosting	96.15	5.739	142.47	1.121	0.5207
Standalone RoBERTa Baseline		**96.69**	160.612	77.94	31.362	14.5701

Table 2: Results of restaurant review dataset on different feature extraction methods.

Product Review Dataset						
Feature Extraction Method	Classifier	Accuracy	Time (min)	Memory (MB)	Energy (Wh)	CO_2 (g.)
BOW	SVM	91.29	0.078	9.75	0.015	0.0071
	Voting	91.29	0.392	10.27	0.077	0.0356
	Boosting	91.05	0.012	8.59	**0.002**	0.0011
TF-IDF	SVM	92.83	0.081	9.90	0.016	0.0074
	Voting	92.08	0.403	10.41	0.079	0.0365
	Boosting	91.57	0.012	8.79	0.003	0.0011
CBOW	SVM	75.88	0.120	14.83	0.023	0.0109
	Voting	78.79	0.432	14.89	0.085	0.0392
	Boosting	80.33	0.094	10.78	0.018	0.0085
FastText	SVM	93.44	**0.010**	7.33	**0.002**	**0.0010**
	Voting	90.73	0.136	7.63	0.027	0.0123
	Boosting	93.39	0.014	**6.82**	0.003	0.0013
DWE	SVM	92.93	2.092	557.20	0.409	0.1899
	Voting	90.91	2.346	554.76	0.459	0.2130
	Boosting	93.82	2.070	551.72	0.405	0.1880
CNN	SVM	92.69	5.717	3297.52	1.117	0.5186
	Voting	92.88	22.072	3326.16	4.324	1.9965
	Boosting	92.04	3.648	2714.40	0.714	0.3306
LSTM	SVM	92.41	6.006	65.20	1.173	0.5452
	Voting	92.97	6.144	65.45	1.200	0.5576
	Boosting	92.88	5.933	64.67	1.159	0.5384
RoBERTa	SVM	84.64	5.352	166.12	1.045	0.4856
	Voting	87.68	6.611	151.27	1.291	0.5998
	Boosting	90.26	5.114	133.97	0.999	0.4640
RoBERTa + FastText	SVM	94.14	6.269	156.73	1.224	0.5688
	Voting	93.49	6.837	156.28	1.335	0.6203
	Boosting	93.53	6.163	146.63	1.221	0.5682
Standalone RoBERTa Baseline		**94.66**	213.961	95.89	41.779	19.4092

Table 3: Results of product review dataset on different feature extraction methods.

Standalone Models						
Dataset	Models	Accuracy	Time (min)	Memory (MB)	Energy (Wh)	CO_2 (g.)
IMDB	CNN-LSTM	88.41	**39.44**	**328.97**	**7.705**	**3.579**
	DistilBERT	89.92	498.29	614.11	97.310	45.207
	RoBERTa	**91.02**	997.88	606.14	201.054	90.554
Restaurant	CNN-LSTM	96.03	**2.27**	**58.33**	**0.444**	**0.206**
	DistilBERT	96.57	76.01	71.18	14.845	6.896
	RoBERTa	**96.69**	160.61	77.94	31.362	14.570
Product	CNN-LSTM	92.13	**2.78**	**60.66**	**0.543**	**0.252**
	DistilBERT	93.89	105.59	91.53	20.621	9.580
	RoBERTa	**94.66**	213.96	95.89	41.779	19.409

Table 4: Results of standalone models on the three datasets.

review dataset. RoBERTa achieves the highest accuracy, while FastText, DWE, and RoBERTa + FastText feature extractors with the SVM classifier achieve nearly the same performance with major carbon emission reductions. DWE with SVM produces 78 times less carbon with only a 0.59% reduction in accuracy when compared to fine-tuned RoBERTa. Similarly, RoBERTa + FastText with SVM and FastText with SVM produce 27 times and 24,283 times less carbon emissions, while only losing 0.16% and 0.68% in accuracy, respectively.

The results from the product review dataset (Table 3) further solidify our observations so far. DWE with boosting, RoBERTa + FastText with SVM, and FastText with SVM result in 103 times, 34 times, and 19,409 times less carbon emissions with only 0.84%, 0.52%, and 1.22% accuracy reduction, respectively, when compared to fine-tuned RoBERTa.

Standalone Models. The results of our standalone models are presented in Table 4. For IMDB review, RoBERTa requires almost 17 hours to complete the task, consuming 201.05 Wh of electricity which produces 90.554g of CO_2. DistilBERT takes almost 9 hours and emits 45.207 g CO_2 which is comparatively much lower than the RoBERTa model.

CNN vs. CNN-LSTM. We also find that using CNN as a feature extractor produces slightly better results than the CNN-LSTM model, though at the cost of higher memory use.[2] For example, in the IMDB review dataset, CNN with the voting ensemble attains 89.65% accuracy whereas the CNN-LSTM standalone model achieves 88.41% accuracy.

[2]We also tried CNN and LSTM as standalone models but the results were worse than the CNN-LSTM model.

6 Conclusion & Future Work

We contextualized the accuracy of sentiment analysis systems within their computing resource requirements: runtime, maximum memory use, energy expenditure, and estimated CO_2 emissions. As expected, a finetuned LLM achieves the highest accuracy in all three datasets. However, this comes at the cost of tens to thousands of times the cost in terms of other resources (time, memory, energy, and CO_2) when compared to other configurations which result in accuracy reductions of less than 1%. We find that the FastText feature extractor with an SVM classifier, in particular, achieves good accuracy scores while having minimal resource requirements.

As such, for the vast majority of use cases, we recommend this configuration (concatenating the frozen RoBERTa embeddings to FastText (RoBERTa+FastText) w/ SVM) where one must balance resource costs with output quality. It provides strong accuracy scores without incurring the extreme time and energy costs of fine-tuning RoBERTa. Although our experiments only considered the task of sentiment analysis, we expect that the major patterns would carry over to other classification tasks to the degree that they have similar dataset features (e.g., text length, dataset size, difficulty, etc.). We encourage others to test this hypothesis and provide insights into which techniques best balance output quality with resource usage in other NLP domains.

Due to our own resource constraints, our experiments do not include the most cutting-edge LLM models (e.g., GPT-3.5, LLaMa, etc.). The use and deployment of these models are qualitatively different (e.g., prompting, RLHF, etc.) from those we considered and thus are outside of the scope of this paper. We leave this extension of our experiments for future work.

Acknowledgements

This project was fully supported by the University of South Florida.

References

Aniruddha Adhikary. 2019. Restaurant reviews in dhaka, bangladesh. `https://www.kaggle.com/tuxboy/restaurant-reviews-in-dhaka-bangladesh`. Accessed: January 12, 2023.

Apoorv Agarwal, Boyi Xie, Ilia Vovsha, Owen Rambow, and Rebecca Passonneau. 2011. Sentiment analysis of twitter data. In *Proceedings of the Workshop on Languages in Social Media*, LSM '11, page 30–38, USA. Association for Computational Linguistics.

Najla M Alharbi, Norah S Alghamdi, Eman H Alkhammash, and Jehad F Al Amri. 2021. Evaluation of sentiment analysis via word embedding and rnn variants for amazon online reviews. *Mathematical Problems in Engineering*, 2021:1–10.

Nesrine Bannour, Sahar Ghannay, Aurélie Névéol, and Anne-Laure Ligozat. 2021. Evaluating the carbon footprint of NLP methods: a survey and analysis of existing tools. In *Proceedings of the Second Workshop on Simple and Efficient Natural Language Processing*, pages 11–21, Virtual. Association for Computational Linguistics.

Piotr Bojanowski, Edouard Grave, Armand Joulin, and Tomas Mikolov. 2016. Enriching word vectors with subword information. *arXiv preprint arXiv:1607.04606*.

Tom Brown, Benjamin Mann, Nick Ryder, Melanie Subbiah, Jared D Kaplan, Prafulla Dhariwal, Arvind Neelakantan, Pranav Shyam, Girish Sastry, Amanda Askell, Sandhini Agarwal, Ariel Herbert-Voss, Gretchen Krueger, Tom Henighan, Rewon Child, Aditya Ramesh, Daniel Ziegler, Jeffrey Wu, Clemens Winter, Chris Hesse, Mark Chen, Eric Sigler, Mateusz Litwin, Scott Gray, Benjamin Chess, Jack Clark, Christopher Berner, Sam McCandlish, Alec Radford, Ilya Sutskever, and Dario Amodei. 2020. Language models are few-shot learners. In *Advances in Neural Information Processing Systems*, volume 33, pages 1877–1901. Curran Associates, Inc.

Tianqi Chen and Carlos Guestrin. 2016. Xgboost: A scalable tree boosting system. In *Proceedings of the 22nd ACM SIGKDD International Conference on Knowledge Discovery and Data Mining*, KDD '16, page 785–794, New York, NY, USA. Association for Computing Machinery.

Datafiniti. 2018. Grammar and online product reviews. `https://data.world/datafiniti/grammar-and-online-product-reviews`. Accessed: January 10, 2023.

Jacob Devlin, Ming-Wei Chang, Kenton Lee, and Kristina Toutanova. 2019. BERT: Pre-training of deep bidirectional transformers for language understanding. In *Proceedings of the 2019 Conference of the North American Chapter of the Association for Computational Linguistics: Human Language Technologies, Volume 1 (Long and Short Papers)*, pages 4171–4186, Minneapolis, Minnesota. Association for Computational Linguistics.

Dionysis Goularas and Sani Kamis. 2019. Evaluation of deep learning techniques in sentiment analysis from twitter data. In *2019 International Conference on Deep Learning and Machine Learning in Emerging Applications (Deep-ML)*, pages 12–17.

M.A. Hearst, S.T. Dumais, E. Osuna, J. Platt, and B. Scholkopf. 1998. Support vector machines. *IEEE Intelligent Systems and their Applications*, 13(4):18–28.

Daniel Hershcovich, Nicolas Webersinke, Mathias Kraus, Julia Bingler, and Markus Leippold. 2022. Towards climate awareness in NLP research. In *Proceedings of the 2022 Conference on Empirical Methods in Natural Language Processing*, pages 2480–2494, Abu Dhabi, United Arab Emirates. Association for Computational Linguistics.

Thanh Lam Hoang, Gabriele Picco, Yufang Hou, Young-Suk Lee, Lam Nguyen, Dzung Phan, Vanessa Lopez, and Ramon Fernandez Astudillo. 2021. Ensembling graph predictions for amr parsing. In *Advances in Neural Information Processing Systems*, volume 34, pages 8495–8505. Curran Associates, Inc.

Armand Joulin, Edouard Grave, Piotr Bojanowski, and Tomas Mikolov. 2017. Bag of tricks for efficient text classification. In *Proceedings of the 15th Conference of the European Chapter of the Association for Computational Linguistics: Volume 2, Short Papers*, pages 427–431, Valencia, Spain. Association for Computational Linguistics.

Alexandre Lacoste, Alexandra Luccioni, Victor Schmidt, and Thomas Dandres. 2019. Quantifying the carbon emissions of machine learning. *Workshop on Tackling Climate Change with Machine Learning at NeurIPS 2019*.

Yinhan Liu, Myle Ott, Naman Goyal, Jingfei Du, Mandar Joshi, Danqi Chen, Omer Levy, Mike Lewis, Luke Zettlemoyer, and Veselin Stoyanov. 2019. Roberta: A robustly optimized BERT pretraining approach. *CoRR*, abs/1907.11692.

Kadan Lottick, Silvia Susai, Sorelle A. Friedler, and Jonathan P. Wilson. 2019. Energy usage reports: Environmental awareness as part of algorithmic accountability. *Workshop on Tackling Climate Change with Machine Learning at NeurIPS 2019*.

Andrew L. Maas, Raymond E. Daly, Peter T. Pham, Dan Huang, Andrew Y. Ng, and Christopher Potts. 2011. Learning word vectors for sentiment analysis.

In *Proceedings of the 49th Annual Meeting of the Association for Computational Linguistics: Human Language Technologies*, pages 142–150, Portland, Oregon, USA. Association for Computational Linguistics.

Tomás Mikolov, Kai Chen, Greg Corrado, and Jeffrey Dean. 2013. Efficient estimation of word representations in vector space. In *1st International Conference on Learning Representations, ICLR 2013, Scottsdale, Arizona, USA, May 2-4, 2013, Workshop Track Proceedings*.

F. Pedregosa, G. Varoquaux, A. Gramfort, V. Michel, B. Thirion, O. Grisel, M. Blondel, P. Prettenhofer, R. Weiss, V. Dubourg, J. Vanderplas, A. Passos, D. Cournapeau, M. Brucher, M. Perrot, and E. Duchesnay. 2011. Scikit-learn: Machine learning in Python. *Journal of Machine Learning Research*, 12:2825–2830.

Matthew E. Peters, Mark Neumann, Mohit Iyyer, Matt Gardner, Christopher Clark, Kenton Lee, and Luke Zettlemoyer. 2018. Deep contextualized word representations. In *Proceedings of the 2018 Conference of the North American Chapter of the Association for Computational Linguistics: Human Language Technologies, Volume 1 (Long Papers)*, pages 2227–2237, New Orleans, Louisiana. Association for Computational Linguistics.

Raj Pranesh and Ambesh Shekhar. 2020. Analysis of resource-efficient predictive models for natural language processing. In *Proceedings of SustaiNLP: Workshop on Simple and Efficient Natural Language Processing*, pages 136–140, Online. Association for Computational Linguistics.

Pranav Rajpurkar, Robin Jia, and Percy Liang. 2018. Know what you don't know: Unanswerable questions for SQuAD. In *Proceedings of the 56th Annual Meeting of the Association for Computational Linguistics (Volume 2: Short Papers)*, pages 784–789, Melbourne, Australia. Association for Computational Linguistics.

Radim Řehůřek and Petr Sojka. 2010. Software Framework for Topic Modelling with Large Corpora. In *Proceedings of the LREC 2010 Workshop on New Challenges for NLP Frameworks*, pages 45–50, Valletta, Malta. ELRA.

Gerard Salton and Christopher Buckley. 1988. Term-weighting approaches in automatic text retrieval. *Information Processing & Management*, 24(5):513–523.

Emma Strubell, Ananya Ganesh, and Andrew McCallum. 2019. Energy and policy considerations for deep learning in NLP. In *Proceedings of the 57th Annual Meeting of the Association for Computational Linguistics*, pages 3645–3650, Florence, Italy. Association for Computational Linguistics.

Romal Thoppilan, Daniel De Freitas, Jamie Hall, Noam Shazeer, Apoorv Kulshreshtha, Heng-Tze Cheng, Alicia Jin, Taylor Bos, Leslie Baker, Yu Du, YaGuang Li, Hongrae Lee, Huaixiu Steven Zheng, Amin Ghafouri, Marcelo Menegali, Yanping Huang, Maxim Krikun, Dmitry Lepikhin, James Qin, Dehao Chen, Yuanzhong Xu, Zhifeng Chen, Adam Roberts, Maarten Bosma, Vincent Zhao, Yanqi Zhou, Chung-Ching Chang, Igor Krivokon, Will Rusch, Marc Pickett, Pranesh Srinivasan, Laichee Man, Kathleen Meier-Hellstern, Meredith Ringel Morris, Tulsee Doshi, Renelito Delos Santos, Toju Duke, Johnny Soraker, Ben Zevenbergen, Vinodkumar Prabhakaran, Mark Diaz, Ben Hutchinson, Kristen Olson, Alejandra Molina, Erin Hoffman-John, Josh Lee, Lora Aroyo, Ravi Rajakumar, Alena Butryna, Matthew Lamm, Viktoriya Kuzmina, Joe Fenton, Aaron Cohen, Rachel Bernstein, Ray Kurzweil, Blaise Aguera-Arcas, Claire Cui, Marian Croak, Ed Chi, and Quoc Le. 2022. Lamda: Language models for dialog applications.

Ian H. Witten, Eibe Frank, and Mark A. Hall. 2011. *Data Mining: Practical Machine Learning Tools and Techniques*, 3rd edition. Morgan Kaufmann Publishers Inc., San Francisco, CA, USA.

Thomas Wolf, Lysandre Debut, Victor Sanh, Julien Chaumond, Clement Delangue, Anthony Moi, Pierric Cistac, Tim Rault, Remi Louf, Morgan Funtowicz, Joe Davison, Sam Shleifer, Patrick von Platen, Clara Ma, Yacine Jernite, Julien Plu, Canwen Xu, Teven Le Scao, Sylvain Gugger, Mariama Drame, Quentin Lhoest, and Alexander Rush. 2020. Transformers: State-of-the-art natural language processing. In *Proceedings of the 2020 Conference on Empirical Methods in Natural Language Processing: System Demonstrations*, pages 38–45, Online. Association for Computational Linguistics.

Xiang Zhang, Junbo Jake Zhao, and Yann LeCun. 2015. Character-level convolutional networks for text classification. *CoRR*, abs/1509.01626.

Mingqiang Zhou, Dan Liu, Yanhui Zheng, Qingsheng Zhu, and Ping Guo. 2022. A text sentiment classification model using double word embedding methods. *Multimedia Tools and Applications*, pages 1–20.

A Data Preprocessing

For data preprocessing, we normalize all the texts by converting them into lowercase, removing URLs, HTML tags, email addresses, non-alphabetic characters, all the special characters, and stop words, tokenizing the text data, and lemmatizing the text. We also transform contractions to their expanded full form to maintain uniformity.

B Abandoned Methods

Early in our experiments, we also considered i) GloVe, ii) Skip-gram, and iii) lower layers (non-

12th) of RoBERTa-base as feature extractors, bagging as a classifier, and ALBERT as a standalone model. However, quite quickly we found that these methods consistently gave poor accuracy results or results that were not qualitatively different from a feature extractor already considered in our experiments.

C Workstation configuration

GPU: RTX 3090 (24GB VRAM); RAM: 32 GB (2x 16GB Corsair CMW32GX4M2Z3600C18); CPU: AMD Ryzen 9 5900X 12-Core Processor.

D Dataset Details

The IMDB movie review is a balanced dataset of 25k samples for each positive and negative label. The restaurant review dataset is collected from 338 restaurants in Dhaka, Bangladesh and the product review dataset is procured from 1,000 different products. These original datasets use 5-star rating systems and we use 1-star samples as negative polarity and all 5-star samples as positive polarity examples. This leads to 8,621 positive reviews and 2,241 negative reviews in the restaurant review dataset. As the product review dataset is highly imbalanced and we seek to investigate the effect of dataset size in our experiments, we further subsample the positive reviews in the product review dataset down to 6,981 positive reviews, while keeping all 3,701 negative reviews.

E Model Parameters Details

Regarding the non-pretrained neural models, we use a dropout rate of 0.2, maximum sequence lengths of 512, and LSTM layers with 128 units. For the restaurant and product review datasets, the vocabulary size of embedding layers is 10,000 and the CNN layers have a kernel size of 3, with 128 filters. For the IMDB review dataset, the kernel size and number of filters in the first convolution layer are 5 and 300, respectively, while those for the second convolution layer are 3 and 100. The size of the vocabulary is 30,000.

Additionally, we also try different parameters of SVM, XGBoost, MNB, and RF but the default one got the more prominent result compared to others. For example, when we use RF in our voting ensemble method, we also try the number of estimators=200, random state=1200, and criterion='entropy'.

The RoBERTa base model comes pretrained with 12 transformer layers, 12 attention heads, and a hidden layer size of 768. DistilBERT base uncased model has 6 layers with 12 attention heads. Other tested hyperparameters for LLMs are represented in Table 5

F Average Result Diagram for Restaurant Review Dataset

Hyperparameter	Tested Values	Optimal Value
Optimizer	Adam, Nadam, SGD	Adam
Epochs	2, 3, 4	3
Learning Rate	1e-1, 5e-1, 2e-1	1e-1
Batch Size	4, 8, 16	8

Table 5: Tested Hyperparameters for LLMs other than Specified Particularly

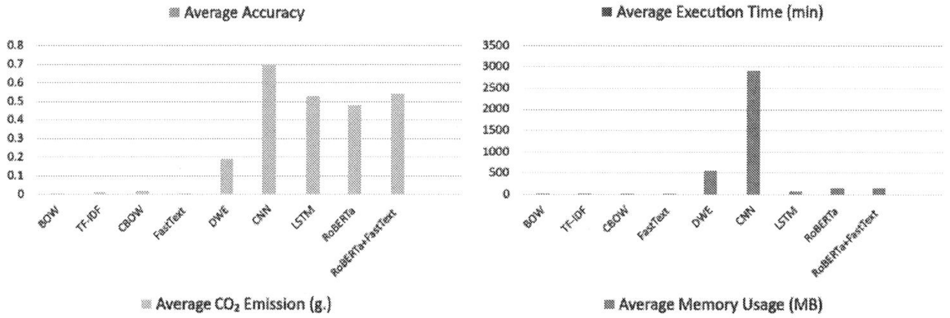

Figure 4: Average Results Diagram of Restaurant Review Dataset

OffMix-3L: A Novel Code-Mixed Dataset in Bangla-English-Hindi for Offensive Language Identification

Dhiman Goswami*, **Md Nishat Raihan***, **Antara Mahmud**
Antonios Anstasopoulos, **Marcos Zampieri**
George Mason University, USA
{dgoswam, mraihan2, amahmud4, antonis, mzampier}@gmu.edu

Abstract

Code-mixing is a well-studied linguistic phenomenon when two or more languages are mixed in text or speech. Several works have been conducted on building datasets and performing downstream NLP tasks on code-mixed data. Although it is not uncommon to observe code-mixing of three or more languages, most available datasets in this domain contain code-mixed data from only two languages. In this paper, we introduce OffMix-3L, a novel offensive language identification dataset containing code-mixed data from three different languages. We experiment with several models on this dataset and observe that BanglishBERT outperforms other transformer-based models and GPT-3.5.

1 Introduction

Code-mixing and code-switching are common linguistic phenomena observed both in speech and text form. While the two terms are often used interchangeably, code-mixing is defined as the use of words or morphemes from multiple languages within a single utterance, sentence, or discourse whereas code-switching refers to the deliberate alternation between multiple languages within the same context (Thara and Poornachandran, 2018). The first case is often spontaneous while the second case is purposeful. However, both are widely observed in bilingual and multilingual communities.

As described in Anastassiou (2017), several social, linguistic, and cognitive factors are behind these two phenomena. Socially, this often serves as a sign of group identity which allows individuals to navigate multiple social and cultural affiliations. Linguistically, it is common for bilingual speakers to not be able to find a word for a specific concept in one language thus using a word from another language to help communication. Additionally, there are several cases even in monolingual communities, when code-mixing might be the convenient way to express a concept as in the case of English loan words such as *feedback* used in various languages.

Most commonly, code-mixing is a bilingual phenomenon. Byers-Heinlein and Lew-Williams (2013), for example, estimates that by the year 2035, over half of children enrolled in kindergarten in California will have grown up speaking a language other than English. Another study conducted by Jeffery and van Beuningen (2020) shows that bilingualism is a common practice in European countries such as Germany and Spain. However, in cosmopolitan cities and areas like New York, London, Singapore, and others, code-mixing with three or more languages is fairly common. This is also observed in countries like Luxembourg, and regions such as West Bengal, and South-East India where more than two languages are commonly used on a daily basis.

Several papers have presented code-mixed datasets for various NLP tasks (KhudaBukhsh et al., 2020; Krishnan et al., 2022). However, most of these datasets are bilingual leaving the processing of code-mixing in three or more languages largely unexplored. In this paper, we present a Bangla-Hindi-English dataset annotated for offensive language identification. To the best of our knowledge, this is one of the first datasets to contain code-mixing between more than two languages.

The main contributions of this paper are as follows:

- We introduce OffMix-3L, a novel three-language code-mixed test dataset in Bangla-Hindi-English for offensive language identification. OffMix-3L contains 1,001 instances annotated by speakers of the three languages. We made OffMix-3L freely available to the community.[1]

*These two authors contributed equally to this work.
WARNING: This paper contains examples that are offensive in nature.

[1]https://github.com/LanguageTechnologyLab/OffMix-3L

Proceedings of the 11th International Workshop on Natural Language Processing for Social Media, pages 21–27
November 1, 2023. ©2023 Association for Computational Linguistics

- We provide a comprehensive evaluation of several monolingual, bilingual, and multilingual models on OffMix-3L.

We present OffMix-3L exclusively as a test set due to the unique and specialized nature of the task. The size of the dataset, while limiting for training purposes, offers a high-quality testing environment with gold-standard labels that will serve as a benchmark in this domain. Given the scarcity of similar datasets and the challenges associated with data collection, OffMix-3L provides an important resource for the rigorous evaluation of offensive language identification models, filling a critical gap in multilevel code-mixing research.

2 Related Work

There have been several studies describing Bangla-English (Alam, 2006; Hasan et al., 2015; Hossain and Bar, 2015; Begum and Haque, 2013; Mahbubul Alam and Quyyum, 2016), Hindi-English (Singh, 1985; Bali et al., 2014; Thara and Poornachandran, 2018) and Bangla-Hindi (Ali et al., 2019; Jose et al., 2020) code-mixing and code-switching separately. Code-mixing between these three languages has also been studied separately in NLP.

There have been few studies conducted on offensive language identification for Bangla-English dode-mixed data. The work by Jahan et al. (2019) focused on detecting Bangla-English code-mixed and transliterated offensive comments on Facebook. Another Bangla-English dataset is gathered by Wadud et al. (2021), where they collected 2,200 instances.

Comparatively more work has been carried out for Hindi-English Code-mixing. Sreelakshmi et al. (2020) uses fastText (Joulin et al., 2016) to represent 10,000 instances collected from different sources. Other offensive language datasets collected from Facebook and Twitter were introduced by Bohra et al. (2018); Kumar et al. (2018); Rani et al. (2020). Mundra and Mittal (2022) proposes Fused Attention-based Network (FA-Net), which introduces a fusion of attention mechanism of collective and mutual learning between local and sequential features for Hindi-English offensive language and hate speech classification. Gupta et al. (2021) uses Character Level Embeddings, GRU, and attention layer to offensive language identification in Hindi-English code-mixed.

To the best of our knowledge, no existing work focuses specifically on Hindi-Bangla code-mixing. However, some studies focused on multiple Indian languages code-mixing altogether including Bangla and Hindi. The work by Vasantharajan and Thayasivam (2021) focuses on offensive language identification in Dravidian languages. A few similar works include Ravikiran and Annamalai (2021); Sai and Sharma (2020); Kumar et al. (2020); Kumari and Singh (2020); Ranasinghe and Zampieri (2021).

In summary, to the best of our knowledge, there has been no work on offensive language identification for code-mixed Bangla-English-Hindi. There have also been no offensive language datasets made available for these three languages. OffMix-3L fills this gap by providing the community with a novel resource for these three languages. OffMix-3L provides the community with the opportunity to evaluate how state-of-the-art models perform on Bangla-English-Hindi.

3 The *OffMix-3L* Dataset

We choose a controlled data collection method, asking the volunteers to freely contribute data in Bangla, English, and Hindi. This decision stems from several challenges of extracting such specific code-mixed data from social media and other online platforms. Our approach ensures data quality and sidesteps the ethical concerns associated with using publicly available online data. Such types of datasets are often used when it is difficult to mine them from existing corpora. As examples, for fine-tuning LLMs on instructions and conversations, semi-natural datasets like Databricks (2023) and Nie (2023) have become popular.

Data Collection A group of 10 undergraduate students fluent in the three languages was asked to prepare 250 to 300 social media posts each. They were allowed to use any language including Bangla, English, and Hindi to prepare posts on several daily topics like politics, sports, education, social media rumors, etc. We also ask them to switch languages if and wherever they feel comfortable doing so. The inclusion of emojis, hashtags, and transliteration was also encouraged. The students had the flexibility to prepare the data as naturally as possible. Upon completion of this stage, we gathered 1,734 samples that contained at least one word or sub-word from each of the three languages using langdetect (Mazzocchi, 2012) an open-sourced Python tool for language identification.

Data Annotation We annotate the dataset in two steps. Firstly, we recruited three students from social science, computer science, and linguistics fluent in the three languages to serve as annotators. They annotated all 1,734 samples with one of the two labels (Non-Offensive and Offensive) with a raw agreement of 63.7%. We then take 1,106 instances, where all three annotators agree on the labels, and use them in a second step. To further ensure high-quality annotation, we recruit a second group of annotators consisting of two NLP researchers fluent in the three languages. After their annotation, we calculate a raw agreement of 91% (Kvålseth, 1989), a Cohen Kappa score of 0.82. After the two stages, we only keep the instances where both annotators agree, and we end up with a total of 1,001 instances. The label distribution is shown in Table 1.

Label	No. of Data	Percentage
Non-Offensive	522	52.15%
Offensive	479	47.85%
Total	1,001	100%

Table 1: Label distribution in OffMix-3L

Dataset Statistics A detailed description of the dataset statistics is provided in Table 2. Since the dataset was generated by people whose first language is Bangla, we observe that the majority of tokens in the dataset are in Bangla. There are several *Other* tokens in the dataset that are not from Bangla, English, or Hindi language. The *Other* tokens in the dataset primarily contain transliterated words as well as emojis and hashtags. Also, there are several misspelled words that have been classified as *Other* tokens too.

	All	Bangla	English	Hindi	Other
Tokens	87,190	31,228	6,690	14,694	34,578
Types	18,787	7,714	1,135	1,413	8,645
Avg	87.10	31.20	6.68	14.68	34.54
Std Dev	20.58	8.60	3.05	5.74	10.98

Table 2: OffMix-3L Data Card. The row *Avg* represents the average number of tokens with its standard deviation in row *Std Dev*.

Synthetic Train and Development Set We present OffMix-3L as a test dataset and we build a synthetic train and development set that contains Code-mixing for Bangla, English, and Hindi. We use two English training datasets annotated with the same labels as OffMix-3L, namely OLID (Zampieri et al., 2019) and SOLID (Rosenthal et al., 2021). We randomly select 100,000 data instances randomly and we carefully choose an equal number of Non-Offensive and Offensive instances. We then use the *Random Code-mixing Algorithm* (Krishnan et al., 2022) and *r-CM* (Santy et al., 2021) to generate the synthetic Code-mixed dataset.

4 Experiments

Monolingual Models We use seven monolingual models for these experiments, five general models, and two task fined-tuned ones. The five monolingual models are DistilBERT (Sanh et al., 2019), BERT (Devlin et al., 2019), BanglaBERT (Kowsher et al., 2022), roBERTa (Liu et al., 2019), HindiBERT (Nick Doiron, 2023). BanglaBERT is trained in only Bangla and HindiBERT on only Hindi while DistilBERT, BERT, and roBERTa are trained in English only. Finally, the two English task fine-tuned models we use are HateBERT and fBERT (Caselli et al., 2021; Sarkar et al., 2021).

Bilingual Models BanglishBERT (Bhattacharjee et al., 2022) and HingBERT (Nayak and Joshi, 2022) are used as bilingual models as they are trained on both Bangla-English and Hindi-English respectively.

Multilingual Models We use mBERT (Devlin et al., 2019) and XLM-R (Conneau et al., 2020) as multilingual models which are respectively trained on 104 and 100 languages including Bangla-English-Hindi. We also use IndicBERT (Kakwani et al., 2020) and MuRIL (Khanuja et al., 2021) which cover 12 and 17 Indian languages, respectively, including Bangla-English-Hindi. We also perform hyper-parameter tuning while using all the models to prevent overfitting.

Prompting We use prompting with GPT-3.5-turbo model (OpenAI, 2023) from OpenAI for this task. We use the API for zero-shot prompting (see Figure 1) and ask the model to label the test set.

Additionally, we run the same experiments separately on synthetic and natural datasets splitting both in a 60-20-20 way for training, evaluating, and testing purposes.

5 Results

In this experiment, synthetic data is used as a training set and natural data is used as the test set. The

Role: "You are a helpful AI assistant. You are given the task of offensive text classification.

Definition: An offensive text is something that upsets or embarrasses people because it is rude or insulting. You will be given a text to label either 'Offensive' or 'Non-Offensive'.

Task: Generate the label for this **"text"** in the following format: *<label> Your_Predicted_Label <\label>*. Thanks."

Figure 1: Sample GPT-3.5 prompt.

F1 scores of monolingual models range from 0.43 to 0.66 where BERT performs the best. mBERT is the best of all the multilingual models with an F1 score of 0.63. Besides, a zero-shot prompting technique on GPT 3.5 turbo provides a 0.57 weighted F1 score. The best task fine-tuned model is HateBERT with the F1 score of 0.60. Among all the models BanglishBERT scores 0.68 which is the best achieved F1 score. These results are available in Table 3.

Models	F1 Score
BanglishBERT	**0.68**
BERT	0.66
mBERT	0.63
HingBERT	0.60
MuRIL	0.60
HateBERT	0.60
fBERT	0.58
roBERTa	0.58
XLM-R	0.57
DistilBERT	0.57
GPT 3.5 Turbo	0.57
BanglaBERT	0.54
IndicBERT	0.55
HindiBERT	0.43

Table 3: Weighted F-1 score for different models: training on synthetic and tested on natural data (OffMix-3L).

We perform the same experiment using synthetic data for training and testing. We present results in Table 4. Here, mBERT and XLM-R with 0.88 F1 scores are the best-performing models.

6 Error Analysis

We observe *Other* tokens in almost 39% of the whole dataset, as shown in Table 2. These tokens occur due to transliteration which poses a challenge for most of the models since not all of the models are pre-trained on transliterated tokens. BanglishBERT did well since it recognizes both Bangla and English tokens. However, the total number of tokens for Hindi-English is less than Bangla-English tokens, justifying HingBERT's inferior performance compared to BanglishBERT (see Table 3). Also, misspelled words and typos are also observed in the datasets, which are, for the most part, unknown tokens for the models, making the task even more difficult. Some examples are available in Appendix A which are classified wrongly by all the models.

Models	Weighted F1 Score
XLM-R	**0.88**
mBERT	**0.88**
BanglishBERT	0.86
BERT	0.83
HingBERT	0.82
IndicBERT	0.82
MuRIL	0.81
fBERT	0.81
HateBERT	0.81
roBERTa	0.80
DistilBERT	0.79
BanglaBERT	0.76
HindiBERT	0.73

Table 4: Weighted F-1 score for different models: training on synthetic and tested on synthetic data.

7 Conclusion and Future Work

In this paper, we presented OffMix-3L, a Bangla-English-Hindi code-mixed offensive language identification dataset containing 1,001 instances. We also created 100,000 synthetic data in the same three languages for training. We evaluated various monolingual models on these two datasets. Our results show that when training on synthetic data and testing on OffMix-3L, BanglishBERT performs the best. When using synthetic data for both training and testing, multilingual models such as mBERT and XLM-R perform well. In the future, we would like to expand OffMix-3L so that it can serve as both training and testing data. Additionally, we are working on pre-training Bangla-English-Hindi trilingual code-mixing models for offensive language identification.

Acknowledgments

We thank the annotators who helped us with the annotation of OffMix-3L. We further thank the anonymous workshop reviewers for their insightful feedback. Antonios Anastasopoulos is generously supported by NSF award IIS-2125466.

Limitations

Although most datasets for the downstream tasks are scraped from social media posts in the real world, in our case these data instances are generated in a semi-natural manner, meaning that they were generated by people but not scraped from social media directly. This was done due to the complexity of extracting contents that contain a specific 3 language code-mixing in them. Also, the dataset is comparatively smaller in size, since it is costly to generate data by a specific set of people who are fluent in all 3 target languages.

Ethics Statement

The dataset introduced in this paper, which centers on the analysis of offensive language in Bangla-English-Hindi code-mixed text, adheres to the ACL Ethics Policy and seeks to make a valuable contribution to the realm of online safety. OffMix-3L serves as an important resource for the moderation of online content, which will make it easier to create safer digital environments. Moreover, the contributors and annotators of the dataset are paid respectable remuneration and also attended two sessions with psychologist before starting and after completing the work to ensure their mental health is not compromised throughout the course of this dataset preparation.

References

Suraiya Alam. 2006. Code-mixing in bangladesh: A case study of non-government white-collar service holders and professionals. *Asian affairs*, 28(4):52–70.

Muhammad Mooneeb Ali, Mazhar Iqbal Ranjha, and Sartaj Fakhar Jillani. 2019. Effects of code mixing in indian film songs. *Journal of Media Studies*, 31(2).

Fotini Anastassiou. 2017. Factors associated with the code mixing and code-switching of multilingual children: An overview. *International Journal of Linguistics, Literature and Culture*, 4(3):13–26.

Kalika Bali, Jatin Sharma, Monojit Choudhury, and Yogarshi Vyas. 2014. i am borrowing ya mixing?" an analysis of english-hindi code mixing in facebook. In *Proceedings of CodeSwitch*.

Most Tasnim Begum and Md Mahmudul Haque. 2013. Code mixing in the ksa: A case study of expatriate bangladeshi and indian esl teachers. *Arab World English Journal*, 4(4).

Abhik Bhattacharjee, Tahmid Hasan, Wasi Ahmad, Kazi Samin Mubasshir, Md Saiful Islam, Anindya Iqbal, M. Sohel Rahman, and Rifat Shahriyar. 2022. BanglaBERT: Language model pretraining and benchmarks for low-resource language understanding evaluation in Bangla. In *Findings of the ACL*.

Aditya Bohra, Deepanshu Vijay, Vinay Singh, Syed Sarfaraz Akhtar, and Manish Shrivastava. 2018. A dataset of hindi-english code-mixed social media text for hate speech detection. In *Proceedings of PEOPLES*.

Krista Byers-Heinlein and Casey Lew-Williams. 2013. Bilingualism in the early years: What the science says. *LEARNing landscapes*, 7(1):95.

Tommaso Caselli, Valerio Basile, Jelena Mitrović, and Michael Granitzer. 2021. HateBERT: Retraining BERT for abusive language detection in English. In *Proceedings of WOAH*.

Alexis Conneau, Kartikay Khandelwal, Naman Goyal, Vishrav Chaudhary, Guillaume Wenzek, Francisco Guzmán, Edouard Grave, Myle Ott, Luke Zettlemoyer, and Veselin Stoyanov. 2020. Unsupervised cross-lingual representation learning at scale. In *Proceedings of ACL*.

Databricks. 2023. Dolly 2.0: An open source, instruction-following large language model. Accessed: 2023-09-10.

Jacob Devlin, Ming-Wei Chang, Kenton Lee, and Kristina Toutanova. 2019. BERT: Pre-training of Deep Bidirectional Transformers for Language Understanding. In *Proceedings of NAACL*.

Vasu Gupta, Vibhu Sehra, Yashaswi Raj Vardhan, et al. 2021. Hindi-english code mixed hate speech detection using character level embeddings. In *Proceedings of ICCMC*.

Md Kamrul Hasan, Mohd Akhand, et al. 2015. Reviewing the challenges and opportunities presented by code switching and mixing in bangla. *Journal of Education and Practice*, 6(1):103–109.

Didar Hossain and Kapil Bar. 2015. A case study in code-mixing among jahangirnagar university students. *International Journal of English and Literature*, 6(7):123–139.

Maliha Jahan, Istiak Ahamed, Md Rayanuzzaman Bishwas, and Swakkhar Shatabda. 2019. Abusive comments detection in bangla-english code-mixed and transliterated text. In *Proceedings of ICIET*.

Jill V Jeffery and Catherine van Beuningen. 2020. Language education in the eu and the us: Paradoxes and parallels. *Prospects*, 48(3-4):175–191.

Navya Jose, Bharathi Raja Chakravarthi, Shardul Suryawanshi, Elizabeth Sherly, and John P McCrae. 2020. A survey of current datasets for code-switching research. In *Proceedings of ICACCS*.

Armand Joulin, Edouard Grave, Piotr Bojanowski, Matthijs Douze, Hervé Jégou, and Tomás Mikolov. 2016. Fasttext.zip: Compressing text classification models. *CoRR*, abs/1612.03651.

Divyanshu Kakwani, Anoop Kunchukuttan, Satish Golla, NC Gokul, Avik Bhattacharyya, Mitesh M Khapra, and Pratyush Kumar. 2020. Indicnlpsuite: Monolingual corpora, evaluation benchmarks and pre-trained multilingual language models for indian languages. In *Findings of the ACL*.

Simran Khanuja, Diksha Bansal, Sarvesh Mehtani, Savya Khosla, Atreyee Dey, Balaji Gopalan, Dilip Kumar Margam, Pooja Aggarwal, Rajiv Teja Nagipogu, Shachi Dave, et al. 2021. Muril: Multilingual representations for indian languages. *arXiv preprint arXiv:2103.10730*.

Ashiqur R KhudaBukhsh, Shriphani Palakodety, and Jaime G Carbonell. 2020. Harnessing code switching to transcend the linguistic barrier. In *Proceedings of IJCAI*.

M Kowsher, Abdullah As Sami, Nusrat Jahan Prottasha, Mohammad Shamsul Arefin, Pranab Kumar Dhar, and Takeshi Koshiba. 2022. Bangla-bert: transformer-based efficient model for transfer learning and language understanding. *IEEE Access*, 10:91855–91870.

Jitin Krishnan, Antonios Anastasopoulos, Hemant Purohit, and Huzefa Rangwala. 2022. Cross-lingual text classification of transliterated hindi and malayalam. In *Proceedings of Big Data*.

Ritesh Kumar, Atul Kr Ojha, Shervin Malmasi, and Marcos Zampieri. 2020. Evaluating aggression identification in social media. In *Proceedings of TRAC*.

Ritesh Kumar, Aishwarya N. Reganti, Akshit Bhatia, and Tushar Maheshwari. 2018. Aggression-annotated Corpus of Hindi-English Code-mixed Data. In *Proceedings of LREC*.

Kirti Kumari and Jyoti Prakash Singh. 2020. Ai_ml_nit_patna@ trac-2: Deep learning approach for multi-lingual aggression identification. In *Proceedings of TRAC*.

Tarald O Kvålseth. 1989. Note on cohen's kappa. *Psychological reports*, 65(1):223–226.

Yinhan Liu, Myle Ott, Naman Goyal, Jingfei Du, Mandar Joshi, Danqi Chen, Omer Levy, Mike Lewis, Luke Zettlemoyer, and Veselin Stoyanov. 2019. Roberta: A robustly optimized BERT pretraining approach. *CoRR*, abs/1907.11692.

Ahmad Mahbub-ul Alam and Shaima Quyyum. 2016. A sociolinguistic survey on code switching & code mixing by the native speakers of bangladesh. *Journal of Manarat International University*, 6(1):8–9.

Daniele Mazzocchi. 2012. langdetect: Language detection library. Python library.

Shikha Mundra and Namita Mittal. 2022. Fa-net: fused attention-based network for hindi english code-mixed offensive text classification. *Social Network Analysis and Mining*, 12(1):100.

Ravindra Nayak and Raviraj Joshi. 2022. L3Cube-HingCorpus and HingBERT: A code mixed Hindi-English dataset and BERT language models. In *Proceedings of WILDRE*.

Nick Doiron. 2023. hindi-bert. Accessed: 2023-09-10.

Jianzhi Nie. 2023. Awesome instruction datasets. Accessed: 2023-09-10.

OpenAI. 2023. Gpt-3.5 turbo fine-tuning and api updates. Accessed: 2023-08-28.

Tharindu Ranasinghe and Marcos Zampieri. 2021. An evaluation of multilingual offensive language identification methods for the languages of india. *Information*, 12(8):306.

Priya Rani, Shardul Suryawanshi, Koustava Goswami, Bharathi Raja Chakravarthi, Theodorus Fransen, and John Philip McCrae. 2020. A comparative study of different state-of-the-art hate speech detection methods in hindi-english code-mixed data. In *Proceedings of TRAC*.

Manikandan Ravikiran and Subbiah Annamalai. 2021. Dosa: Dravidian code-mixed offensive span identification dataset. In *Proceedings of TRAC*.

Sara Rosenthal, Pepa Atanasova, Georgi Karadzhov, Marcos Zampieri, and Preslav Nakov. 2021. SOLID: A large-scale semi-supervised dataset for offensive language identification. In *Findings of the ACL*.

Siva Sai and Yashvardhan Sharma. 2020. Siva@ hasoc-dravidian-codemix-fire-2020: Multilingual offensive speech detection in code-mixed and romanized text. In *Proceedings of FIRE*.

Victor Sanh, Lysandre Debut, Julien Chaumond, and Thomas Wolf. 2019. Distilbert, a distilled version of BERT: smaller, faster, cheaper and lighter. In *Proceedings of EMC2*.

Sebastin Santy, Anirudh Srinivasan, and Monojit Choudhury. 2021. Bertologicomix: How does code-mixing interact with multilingual bert? In *Proceedings of AdaptNLP*.

Diptanu Sarkar, Marcos Zampieri, Tharindu Ranasinghe, and Alexander Ororbia. 2021. fBERT: A neural transformer for identifying offensive content. In *Findings of the ACL*.

Rajendra Singh. 1985. Grammatical constraints on code-mixing: Evidence from hindi-english. *Canadian Journal of Linguistics/Revue canadienne de linguistique*, 30(1):33–45.

K Sreelakshmi, B Premjith, and KP Soman. 2020. Detection of hate speech text in hindi-english code-mixed data. *Procedia Computer Science*, 171:737–744.

S Thara and Prabaharan Poornachandran. 2018. Code-mixing: A brief survey. In *Proceedings of ICACCI*.

Charangan Vasantharajan and Uthayasanker Thayasivam. 2021. Hypers@ dravidianlangtech-eacl2021: Offensive language identification in dravidian code-mixed youtube comments and posts. In *Proceedings of DravidianLangTech*.

Md Anwar Hussen Wadud, Md Abdul Hamid, Muhammad Mostafa Monowar, and Atif Alamri. 2021. L-boost: Identifying offensive texts from social media post in bengali. *Ieee Access*, 9:164681–164699.

Marcos Zampieri, Shervin Malmasi, Preslav Nakov, Sara Rosenthal, Noura Farra, and Ritesh Kumar. 2019. SemEval-2019 task 6: Identifying and categorizing offensive language in social media (OffensEval). In *Proceedings of SemEval*.

A Examples of Misclassified Instances

<u>Non-Offensive:</u> আই এম এক্সসাইটেড টু পার্টিসিপেট টু এ বুক ক্লাব টু শেয়ার মাই আইডিয়াস! এটি amazing যে কীভাবে একটি book মানুষকে একত্রিত করতে পারে এবং meaningful কথাপেকথন শুরু করতে পারে। I am looking forward to hearing ভিন্নধর্মী opinions and অনুধাবন of the book, and learning from others यह मेरी पठन सूची का विस्तार करने और नए लेखकों और शैलियों को खोजने का भी एक शानदार तरीका है। mera maanana hai ki padhana seekhane aur aatm–khoj kee kabhee na khatm hone vaalee yaatra hai #bookclub #discussiongroup

<u>Offensive:</u> The proliferation of young people creating adult content on social media is a reflection of the harmful and unrealistic messages we are sending to our youth about যৌনতা। हमें इन मानदंडों को चुनौती देनी चाहिए और कामुकता के अधिक सशक्त और समावेशी दृष्टिकोण को बढ़ावा देना चाहिए fantasy জগত থেকে তাদের বাস্তবে আসা উচিত har din tiktok karne ka natija #obscence #boycottAdultContent

An Emotion-Enriched and Psycholinguistic Features-Based Approach for Rumor Detection on Online Social Media

Asimul Haque
Department of Computer Science
South Asian University
New Delhi-68, India
asimulhaque@gmail.com

Muhammad Abulaish, SMIEEE
Department of Computer Science
South Asian University
New Delhi-68, India
abulaish@sau.int

Abstract

Social media platforms and online communication tools, once lauded as sources of information, unity, and global connectivity, are now breeding grounds for the unprecedented spread of false, misleading, and manipulative information. Rumor is one type of such information. It consists of untrue information and deceptive messages and is constructed to manipulate emotions. Consequently, emotions are crucial in determining the veracity of rumors. In this paper, we introduce an emotion-enhanced and psycholinguistic features-based approach for rumors detection on social social media. It entails detecting rumors utilizing lexicons and various linguistic features-based learning approaches, primarily by extracting the psychological association of words with their emotions. Emotional and psycholinguistic features are extracted from both posts and comments to enhance the approach and make rumor detection more effective. Using word-level GloVe embedding, the semantic relationships between a post and its comments and their underlying emotions are preserved. The proposed method is evaluated on the popular PHEME dataset and compared to various baselines and SOTA methods, demonstrating substantially superior performance for rumor detection on social media platforms.

1 Introduction

The advent and rapid growth of social media enables users to construct, facilitate, and create connections through the exchange of ongoing ideas, emotions, thoughts, and experiences (Zubiaga et al., 2018; Zhou and Zafarani, 2020). Some individuals acquire information, while others use it to publish and disseminate rumors or false narratives. This rumor continues to spread unchecked across social media platforms, posing numerous explicit and implicit threats to social stability and public trust (Zubiaga et al., 2018). Different manifestations of rumors make their detection a growing concern and necessitate a refined approach to addressing them. During the COVID-19 pandemic, it was observed that thousands of rumors proliferated on social media, ranging from the origin of the corona virus to its cures. For example, the nature of rumor in India differs from that in the West. In India, claims ranged from immunity to natural remedies, whereas in the West, anti-vaccine arguments garnered popularity[1]. Recently, misinformation and propaganda regarding the Ukraine war and France unrest have circulated on social media[2]. Social media posts are intentionally created to delude and elicit strong emotions in users in order to spread them across the network. The information published online has real-world consequences. False information spreads more quickly if it is disseminated, as demonstrated by the authors in (Vosoughi et al., 2018).

Numerous fact-checking websites, such as Snopes, PolitiFact, and FactCheck, manually evaluate the accuracy of claims. For instance, PolitiFact evaluates claims using a Truth-O-Meter that indicates the relative accuracy of a statement. To combat misinformation, more than simply manual fact-checking is required. It requires adaptability on multiple fronts, including social media platform regulation, media literacy programs, and the adoption of advanced emerging tools in a responsible manner, in order to address the issue on a large scale. Various governments, international and regional organizations have adopted numerous strategies to combat rumors and fake news on a global scale. For example, (i) the United Nations exhorted users to exercise caution prior to sharing. During the COVID-19 infodemic, social media users were encouraged to consider the 5W's; *Who made it, what is the source of informa-*

[1] http://www.globaltimes.cn/content/1178157.shtml
[2] http://www.bbc.com/news/world-europe-66081671

Proceedings of the 11th International Workshop on Natural Language Processing for Social Media, pages 28–37
November 1, 2023.

tion, where did it come from, why are you sharing this, and *when was it published*[3]? (ii) the European Union has devised a self-regulatory code of conduct and imposed content moderation requirements on social media platforms such as `Facebook` and `YouTube`, (iii) Singapore has enacted stringent criminal laws to combat online misinformation, (iv) India is combating the proliferation of online misinformation through the Digital India Bill[4]. The evolving hazards are further complicated by technological advances such as `ChatGPT` and `Generative AI`. Automatic detection of rumors is a formidable challenge for the research community and an essential requirement for contemporary society. The varying degrees of falsified information used to deceive users make it more difficult to find a method to prevent the spread of rumors that undermine trust in the social media ecosystem.

In this paper, we relate the psychological theories indicating that users with malicious intent exhibit uncertainty, vagueness, emotion, and indirect forms of expression, whereas trusted users cite primary sources more frequently (Buller and Burgoon, 1996). It has also been observed in the literature that some people use simple words to express their emotions on social media platforms, while others prefer exaggerated and provocative language (Rashkin et al., 2017). In addition, researchers are investigating the representation of emotion and sentiment as structural properties for disseminating false information (Pröllochs et al., 2021; Martel et al., 2020). We augment these works in order to identify the combinations of feature sets that yield the best predictive capabilities for rumors classification. We intend to demonstrate the effectiveness of emotion-related features and combine them with psycholinguistic features in order to facilitate classification tasks. The extraction of emotion-related features is facilitated by lexicons developed by researchers to aid in emotion analysis (Mohammad and Turney, 2013; Mohammad, 2018). The word-level `GloVe` embedding (Pennington et al., 2014) is also used to determine the semantic affinities of posts and comments with their underlying emotion words. Despite the fact that emotion is a key factor in rumor propagation, the scholarly community has paid little attention to comprehending the prevalence of emotions in online posts and comments and their usefulness in detecting rumors.

[3] `https://news.un.org/en/story/2020/06/1067422`

[4] `https://indianexpress.com/article/opinion/columns/india-show-way-combatting-fake-news-global-south-8646961/`

This paper employs emotions for rumor detection by defining two emotion categories for social media posts: *post emotion* and *comment emotion*. We provide the features for the rumor detection framework by capturing and analyzing the user's emotions when publishing social media posts and the user's reactive emotions when the posts reach them. The numerous emotion-related expressions of social media posts and comments are analyzed, and a straightforward and persuasive approach is proposed, taking into account emotion and sentiment polarities that investigate their aspects in rumor detection. The following is a summary of the main contributions of this paper:

- Presenting techniques for extracting emotion-related features from social media posts and comments and integrating them with their psycholinguistic and syntactic features.
- Introducing an emotion-enhanced and psycholinguistic features-based approach for detecting rumors on social media that combines emotion-related aspects, psycholinguistic features, and a word embedding model.
- An empirical study using the popular `PHEME` dataset to assess the efficacy of emotion-enhanced and psycholinguistic features-based approaches for rumor detection.

The remaining parts of the paper are organized as follows. Section 2 presents a brief review of the related literature. Section 3 presents the architectural and functional details of the proposed approach. Section 4 presents the dataset, experimental results, and comparative analysis of the proposed approach. Finally, Section 5 concludes the paper and presents future research directions.

2 Related Works

There are two widely accepted theories on basic emotion models based on psychological science (Plutchik, 1982; Ekman, 1992). The study of emotions and their implications gets the interest of several fields, especially affective computing (Picard, 2000), where the emotions and sentiments of words and phrases are analyzed. Emotion analysis frequently resembles sentiment analysis and opinion mining, as well as the study of affective lexicons in psycholinguistics, which assesses the connection between psychological processes and linguistic behaviors (Pang et al., 2008). In contrast to opinion mining and sentiment analysis, emotion analysis is not limited to analyzing the polarity but also associating text with a predefined set of psychological terms determined by dimensions such as valence, arousal, and dominance (Russell, 2003).

There are recent works on determining the veracity of rumors; however, very few were focused on detecting rumors based on emotion-related features. Vosoughi et al. (2018) explored emotions in rumors on social media and found that true rumors contain *joy, sadness, trust, and anticipation*, whereas false rumors trigger *fear, disgust*, and *surprise*. Ajao et al. (2019) determined the relationship between fake news and the sentiments of the social media posts. Giachanou et al. (2019) proposed an approach based on an LSTM neural network, which incorporates emotional signals to differentiate between credible and non-credible claims. Abulaish et al. (2019) incorporated sentimental aspects through a graph-based approach using POS tags to identify anxious and doubtful terms for rumor detection. Wasi and Abulaish (2020) proposed a logistic regression-based sentiment classification approach that uses prior domain knowledge extracted from a lexicon and unlabeled domain data.

Dong et al. (2022) proposed a method for fake news detection based on hypergraph attention networks, which employed two hypergraphs to model news contents and user comments to capture high-order relations between words in a news document and comments with the same sentimental polarity. Haque and Abulaish (2022) proposed a graph-based contextual and semantic learning approach using posts and comments to understand the underlying linguistic patterns that exploited the textual and latent information. Xu et al. (2022) studied the role of comments in rumor detection and proposed a method that extracted the features from the original post and associated comments. Choudhry et al. (2022) annotated fake news and rumor datasets with their emotion labels using transfer learning. They proposed a multitasking framework for fake news and rumor detection, predicting the text's emotion and legitimacy. In (Kumari et al., 2021) and (Gupta et al., 2022), the authors investigated the performance improvement of fake news detection with joint learning of novelty, emotion, and sentiments.

Researchers have also explored the misinformation and emotions related to COVID-19 and studied their impacts on the pandemic (Caceres et al., 2022; Gupta et al., 2022; Sosea et al., 2022). Bhardwaj and Abulaish (2023) collected and annotated a large-scale, multi-labeled emotion and sentiment classification dataset that contains COVID-19-related textual data. They analyzed user sentiments and emotions expressed in tweets during the third wave of the omicron sub-variant pandemic. Furthermore, some researchers have explored different emotional patterns for analyzing various forms of false information, such as hoaxes, propaganda, clickbait, and satire (Rashkin et al., 2017; Ghanem et al., 2020; Mackey et al., 2021).

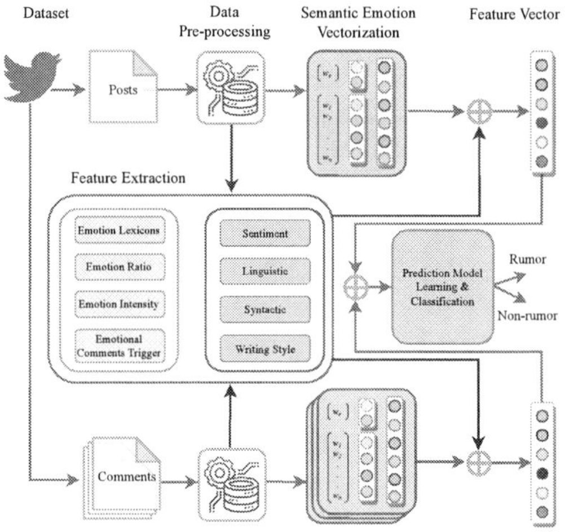

Figure 1: Work-flow of the proposed approach

3 Proposed Approach

In this section, we explain the proposed rumor detection approach and its functional module. The work-flow of the proposed approach for rumor detection is represented in Figure 1.

3.1 Rumor Detection Formalization

Following the state-of-the-art approaches, we consider rumor detection as a binary classification problem. Given any i^{th} social media post p_i and its set of comments $C_{p_i} = \{c_1^{p_i}, c_2^{p_i}, ..., c_m^{p_i}\}$, where $p_i, C_{p_i} \in P$ of a social media dataset P, a rumor function f_x predict whether a post p_i is a rumor or non-rumor. Further, it is defined as f_x: (p, C_p) $\rightarrow \{0, 1\}$ such that,

$$f_x(p, C_p) = \begin{cases} 1, & p \text{ is a rumor} \\ 0, & \text{non-rumor.} \end{cases} \quad (1)$$

3.2 Data Preprocessing

In this step, data preprocessing tasks, such as tokenization, cleaning, and normalization, are conducted on the Twitter dataset. All the posts and comments are tokenized with white space. In normalization, we replace the Twitter-specific tokens, i.e., *hashtags, urls, retweets*, and *mentions*, with the tags ≺*hashtags*≻, ≺*urls*≻, ≺*retweets*≻, and ≺*mentions*≻, respectively. Emojis or emoticons are essential to convey emotion and are frequently used in informal text; therefore, we included them in our dataset by converting them into text using the Python demoji module.

3.3 Emotion Recognition

Trusted or genuine posts retain their natural way of writing without affecting the opinion of users. In contrast, rumorous posts are usually presented in a manner that manipulates emotions using the advantage of arousal and sensitive behaviors of users. Social media posts with emotional words such as astonishment, anger, and anxiety have a broader scope to get viral (Vosoughi et al., 2018). The nature of emotions in posts and comments varies based on social media users' intentions, content, and writing styles. Generally, emotions of posts and comments resonate in cases of outrage and anxiety, whereas, sometimes, posts having neutral feelings raise doubt and fear in their comments (Pröllochs et al., 2021; Vosoughi et al., 2018). Given any i^{th} post p_i and its comments C_{p_i}, the expression of emotions are categorized as post emotion and comments emotion, for which the emotion-related features are extracted to generate features vector $\mathcal{F}_e$.

Post emotion contains emotion-related information about the source post. It focuses on the users' emotions while posting any post on social media. Malign users intentionally feed intense emotions in social media posts to exploit the sensitive behavior of users. Purposefully, they depict themselves as genuine in publishing false but convincing news on controversial topics. We define the post emotion as $post_{emo} \in \mathcal{R}^{\mathcal{F}_e}$, where $\mathcal{R}^{\mathcal{F}_e}$ is the feature space of emotion-related feature $\mathcal{F}_e$.

Comments emotions are reactive emotions that capture emotion-related details from comments. Users commonly get deceived by the provocative emotion fed in the content of source posts and start commenting based on preconceived ideas and aroused feelings. Similarly, as a post, we define comments emotion as $comment_{emo} \in \mathcal{R}^{\mathcal{F}_e}$, where $\mathcal{R}^{\mathcal{F}_e}$ is the feature space of emotion-related feature $\mathcal{F}_e$.

3.4 Emotion-Related Feature Extraction

This section assesses several emotion resources to analyze and extract the range of emotion-related features from the text. Posts and comments are in textual form, represented as textual input $T = \{w_1, w_2, ..., w_n\}$. The following processes are considered to extract the emotion-related features for the textual input T.

3.4.1 Emotion Lexicon

Rumors evoke certain emotions in users; consequently, we consider eight types of emotions based on Plutchik's wheel (Plutchik, 2001) to investigate rumors, i.e., *anger, fear, disgust, trust, sadness, joy, anticipation*, and *surprise*. We use NRC Word-Emotion Association Lexicon (Mohammad and Turney, 2013) for extraction of the emotion categories that persist in the textual input. The emotion categories in the dictionary are represented as $E = \{e_1, e_2, ..., e_r\}$, where r is the total number of emotion categories. The frequency of emotion words belonging to each emotion category for a textual input T is computed using equation 2, where $f_{(T,e_i)}$ is the occurrence of the emotion words of T in a category e_i and $emo_{lex}(w_j, e_i)$ counts if a word w_j, $\forall w_j \in T$ is present in a emotion category e_i.

$$f_{(T,e_i)} = freq\{emo_{lex}(w_j, e_i)\}, \forall e_i \in E \quad (2)$$

Finally, the emotion lexicon feature vector $lex_{(T)}$ for textual input T is expressed by equation 3.

$$lex_{(T)} = \left[f_{(T,e_1)}, f_{(T,e_2)}, ..., f_{(T,e_r)}\right] \quad (3)$$

3.4.2 Emotion Ratio

We evaluate the emotional alignment of the posts and comments toward positive and negative emotion cues. Malign users make complicated stories and allude to negative words more frequently (Vosoughi et al., 2018). As determined in (Ajao et al., 2019), the fraction measure of emotion words at the sentence level is calculated to assess the influence toward positive or negative emotional states. For this purpose, unigrams of input text are matched with the existing lexicon dictionary (Mohammad and Turney, 2013) that counts the number of positive and negative emotions. The consideration of the emotion ratio feature $\mathcal{ER}$ is defined by equation 4, where $freq(e^+, T)$ and

$freq(e^-, T)$ counts the frequency of positive and negative emotions in textual input T, respectively.

$$\mathcal{ER}_{(T)} = \frac{freq(e^-, T)}{freq(e^+, T) + 1}, \forall e^-, e^+ \in E \quad (4)$$

3.4.3 Emotion Intensity

People used to express false narratives with higher intensities to emphasize and arouse intense emotions in the users (Pröllochs et al., 2021). Each word in posts and comments signifies diverse emotion-related signals based on their intensity levels. The `NRC Emotion Intensity Lexicon` (Mohammad, 2018) is used for calculating the emotion intensity score, which contains the same emotion categories considered in Section 3.4.1, with a real-valued score representing that particular word's intensity. We compute the intensity score corresponding to each emotion category by summing the intensity values of emotion words belonging to that category. The emotion intensity feature is defined by equation 5, where $emo_{int}(w_j, e_i)$ is the intensity of a word w_j in an emotion category e_i.

$$int_{(T,e_i)} = \sum_{w_j \in T}^{|T|} emo_{int}(w_j, e_i), \forall e_i \in E \quad (5)$$

The final emotion intensity feature vector $\mathcal{EI}_{(T)}$ for textual input T is obtained by equation 6.

$$\mathcal{EI}_{(T)} = \left[int_{(T,e_1)}, int_{(T,e_2)}, ..., int_{(T,e_r)}\right] \quad (6)$$

3.4.4 Triggered Emotional Comments

Social media users' sensitive and responsive behavior drives them to trigger their emotions after seeing provocating or controversial messages (Giachanou et al., 2018; Martel et al., 2020). They tend to reply or react in emotionalized ways. We incorporated the triggered emotions in comments using counts of their emotional expressions. Accordingly, the calculation is conducted to count the number of comments having positive and negative emotional words. We flag if positive e^+ and negative e^- emotions are present in the textual input T. In the end, for a post p_i the frequency of its flagged comments of C_{p_i} is counted using equation 7.

$$\mathcal{CT}_{(T)} = \left[freq(c, e^+), freq(c, e^-)\right], \forall e^+, e^- \in E \quad (7)$$

Eventually, the emotion-related feature vector $\mathcal{F}_e$ for an input text T is obtained by concatenating the feature vectors generated above, expressed by equation 8.

$$\mathcal{F}_e = lex_{(T)} \oplus \mathcal{ER}_{(T)} \oplus \mathcal{EI}_{(T)} \oplus \mathcal{CT}_{(T)} \quad (8)$$

3.5 Seed Feature Extraction

People cultivate rumors using exaggerated words such as superlatives, subjective, assertive, hedge, and manner adverbs (Wilson et al., 2005; Ott et al., 2011); subjective words are used to dramatize or sensationalize, whereas hedge words indicate vagueness, mystifying, and obscuring language (Islam et al., 2020). Also, mistrust toward online information evokes skepticism and doubt in users (Martel et al., 2020). Beyond emotions, these words need to be focused to enhance the framework's efficiency. We use lexical resources from existing works in communication theory and stylistic analysis of computational linguistics to extract these words from social media posts to characterize between rumor and non-rumor. The following features are comprised in that direction to extract the seed feature vector for the input text T.

Linguistic features: Analyze the psycholinguistic patterns in the text that are incorporated through the score of subjective, aggressive, hateful, and hedging words. Lexicons from (Islam et al., 2020) are used for hedge words to calculate the hedge score for an input text. We also used `LIWC` (Pennebaker et al., 2015), a linguistic dictionary widely used in social science studies composed of $6,400$ (approx.) words with different categories to extract psycholinguistic patterns. We consider categories, i.e., *total pronouns, common adverbs, common adjectives, comparisons, affective processes, negations, anger, sadness, positive emotion, negative emotion, anxiety*, and *swear* words. The subjectivity of an input text is obtained using the total number of words present in an input text by limiting the word count to 15 as an empirically calculated threshold. A transformer-based `Python` library for SocialNLP tasks described in (Pérez et al., 2021) is used for measuring hateful and aggressive scores. In the end, these measures are concatenated to construct a linguistic feature vector $\mathcal{L}_f(T)$.

Sentiment scores: Capture underlying sentimental signals of messages conveyed on social media. Rumorous posts manifest a higher negative sentiment than genuine posts (Vosoughi et al., 2018). To determine the sentiment expressed in an input text, we use the VADER (Hutto and Gilbert, 2014), a lexicon and rule-based sentiment analysis tool devised explicitly for sentiments expressed in microblogs with four dimensions, i.e., *positive, negative, neutral*, and *compound*. We select *positive, negative* and *neutral* sentiment polarity and construct the sentiment score $\mathcal{S}_s(T)$.

Syntactic features: Role are vital from the inception of the literature on rumor identification. The POS tagging is applied using spaCy to extract syntactic features based on the presence of *noun (NN), verb (VB), adverb (RB)*, and *adjective (JJ)* tags along with their fine-grained tags, i.e., *comparative adjective (JJR), superlative adjective (JJS), comparative adverb (RBR), superlative adverb (RBS)*, and *personal pronoun (PRP)*. The tokenized input text is assigned with respective POS tags using Penn Treebank for designing syntactic feature $\mathcal{S}_f(T)$.

Writing style: Include features of users' writing manners that contribute significantly to propagating false and ambiguous information, i.e., the use of punctuations $\{?, !, ...\}$, capital letters, and uppercase words. We consider the count of these measures when they appear in the input text T to construct the feature vector $\mathcal{W}_f(T)$. Finally, the seed feature vector $\mathcal{F}_s$ for the input text T is obtained by concatenating all extracted features, expressed by equation 9.

$$\mathcal{F}_s = \mathcal{L}_f(T) \oplus \mathcal{S}_s(T) \oplus \mathcal{S}_f(T) \oplus \mathcal{W}_f(T) \quad (9)$$

3.6 Semantic Emotion Vectorization

Text embedding, which provides learned word representation as low-dimension dense vectors in continuous embedding space, is applied to preserve the semantic relation of the posts and comments. We employed two embedding tasks, one for document representation and the second for underlying emotion representation in an input text. The emotion representation analyzes the intrinsic emotion in the input text T. It is attained by embedding the most frequent emotion word of the input text using the same embedding model. The textual input T of length n is represented as vector $[v_1, v_2, ..., v_n]$ where $v_i \in \mathcal{R}^d$; $\mathcal{R}^d$ is a d-dimensional word embedding vector for the ith word in the textual input T. For this purpose, we use publicly available 100-dimensional word-level pre-trained GloVe embedding vectors trained over a Twitter dataset with 27 billion tokens[5]. Similarly, we construct the emotion embedding vector $[v_e]$ for the most frequent emotion word with the same embedding model. When extracting the most frequent emotion word, in the case where more than one occurrence appears, we consider the most intensified emotional word based on intensity score. Finally, the emotionalized embedding feature vector $\mathcal{F}_{sv}$ is obtained as the mean of both the embedding vectors defined by equation 10.

$$\mathcal{F}_{sv} = \frac{\sum_1^n [v_i] + [v_e]}{n+1} \forall v_i, v_e \in \mathcal{R}^d \quad (10)$$

Table 1: Statistics of the dataset

Events Name	Posts	Comments	Rumors	Non-Rumors	Total
Charlie Hebdo	2,079	36,189	458	1,621	38,268
Sydney Siege	1,221	22,775	522	699	23,996
Ferguson	1,143	23,032	284	859	24,175
Ottawa Shooting	890	11,394	470	420	12,284
Germanwings Crash	469	4,020	238	231	4,489
Putin Missing	238	597	126	112	835
Prince Toronto	233	669	229	4	902
Gurlitt	138	41	61	77	179
Ebola Essien	14	212	14	0	226
Total	6,425	98,929	2,402	4,023	105,354

3.7 Feature Vector Generation

In this step, the feature vectors for posts and comments are generated using the above-described extraction techniques. The posts and comments are treated concurrently since comments have different emotion-related features and linguistic information depending on the crowd's moods and interest in the ongoing events. Each statistical feature is calculated as a normalized sum of their score. All the above features are extracted for a post p_i and its comments $C_{p_i} = \{c_1^{p_i}, c_2^{p_i}, ..., c_m^{p_i}\}$. Feature vector associated with C_{p_i} is calculated as an average of all $\{C_{p_i}\}_1^m$. The final feature vector $\mathcal{FV}$ is obtained by concatenating the features of a post, i.e., $post_f = \mathcal{F}_e^p \oplus \mathcal{F}_s^p \oplus \mathcal{F}_{sv}^p$ and its comments, i.e., $comments_f = \mathcal{F}_e^c \oplus \mathcal{F}_s^c \oplus \mathcal{F}_{sv}^c$ using equation 11.

$$\mathcal{FV} = post_f \oplus comments_f \quad (11)$$

4 Experimental Setup and Results

In this section, we describe the experimental setup, results, and comparative analysis of the proposed approach with the baseline methods and state-of-the-art approaches. The effectiveness of the proposed approach is evaluated using the evaluation matrix described below.

4.1 Dataset

We conduct our experiment on a publicly available PHEME dataset used in (Kochkina et al., 2018). The dataset contains a collection of posts with their

[5]https://nlp.stanford.edu/projects/glove/

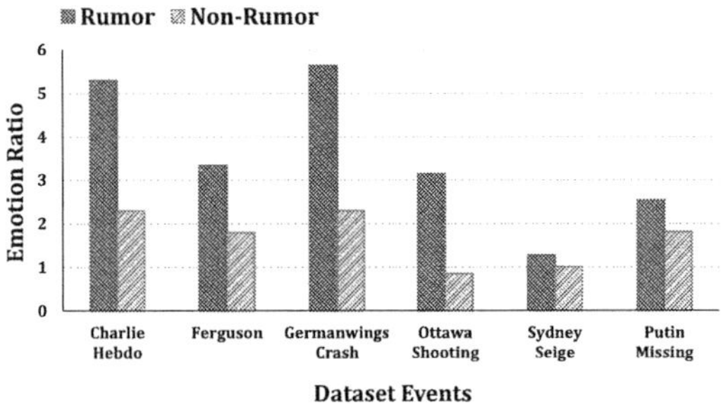

Figure 2: The distribution of negative and positive emotion words in the dataset represented by their ratio

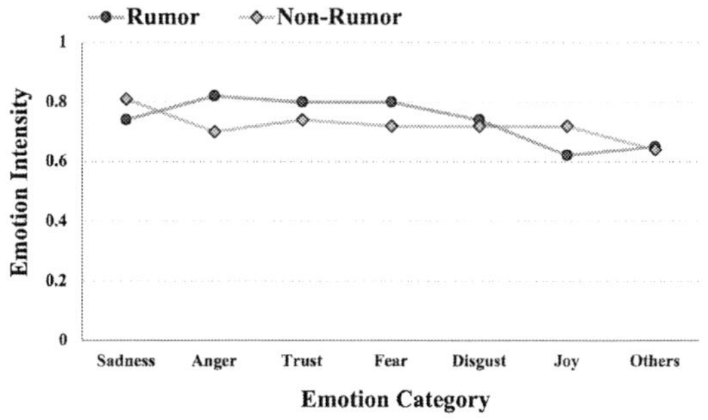

Figure 3: The distribution of emotion words based on their intensity scores in the dataset under the various emotion categories

comments related to nine events posted on `Twitter` during breaking news. The detailed dataset statistics are presented in Table 1.

4.2 Dataset Analysis

This section discusses the analysis of the dataset. The emotion expressed in the dataset varies since people have different expression styles according to their language, culture, and interest in ongoing topics. There are nine events in the dataset; the events containing at least 100 posts of rumor and non-rumor are considered for analysis. Figure 2 shows the presence of negative and positive emotions in the six events of the dataset using their emotion ratio. Figure 3 shows the distribution of emotion words based on their intensity scores under various emotion categories. The analysis also found that the proportion of negative emotions is higher in the rumor compared to non-rumor. Moreover, Emotion words present in the comments of rumor and non-rumor are analyzed, and it was found that the severity of anger, doubt, and fear is much greater in rumors. Extreme forms of words are deliberately chosen to unleash anger, such as deadly, brutal, and hatred.

4.3 Evaluation Metrics

This section discusses performance evaluation metrics for classification. The standard evaluation metrics- *Precision (P), Recall (R)*, and *F1-score* are defined in equations 12, 13, and 14, respectively. The evaluation metrics are defined using the concepts of *true-positive (tp), false-positive (fp)*, and *false-negative (fn). True-positive* is the total number of rumors specified as rumors class correctly; *fp* is the total number of non-rumors specified as rumors; *fn* is the number of rumors identified as non-rumors. *Precision* assesses the correctness, whereas *Recall* evaluates the completeness of coverage of the classifier. Meanwhile, the *F1-score* uses harmonic means to provide a way to combine the contribution of both *Precision* and *Recall* evenly.

$$P = \frac{tp}{tp + fp} \tag{12}$$

$$R = \frac{tp}{tp + fn} \tag{13}$$

$$F1 - score = \frac{2 \times P \times R}{P + R} \tag{14}$$

4.4 Evaluation Results and Comparative Analysis

We performed experiments for the evaluation of the proposed approach using machine learning classification algorithms – *Support Vector Machine (SVM), Gradient Boosting (GB), Logistic Regression (LR)*, and *Multi-layer Perceptron (MLP)*, implemented using the `scikit-learn` `Python` library with the default parameter settings.

The proposed approach is compared with the following baseline methods and state-of-the-art approaches for evaluating the significance of extracted features:

Baseline 1: In this method, only posts are considered to evaluate the significance of emotion-related and seed features.

Baseline 2: In this method, posts and comments are considered to evaluate the seed features only.

Baseline 3: In this method, posts and comments are considered to evaluate the emotion-related features only.

Table 2: Comparative performance evaluation results of our proposed approach with the state-of-the-art approaches and baseline methods

Approach	SVM			LR			GB			MLP		
	P	R	F1	P	R	F1	P	R	F1	P	R	F1
Baseline 1	58.48	50.74	54.33	59.10	55.21	57.08	64.61	66.86	65.71	69.09	65.35	67.16
Baseline 2	70.19	66.35	68.21	69.20	67.32	68.24	72.32	73.34	72.82	75.00	77.71	76.33
Baseline 3	87.42	90.60	88.98	82.49	78.40	80.39	86.34	89.56	87.92	84.38	91.50	87.79
Baseline 4	70.62	66.66	68.58	66.49	69.92	68.16	71.43	72.69	72.05	71.31	70.25	70.77
Abulaish et al. (2019)	41.30	45.56	43.32	40.80	41.93	41.11	56.26	55.40	55.82	64.62	60.10	62.28
Ajao et al. (2019)	87.18	86.00	86.58	84.63	84.88	84.75	85.28	86.82	86.04	88.83	87.21	88.01
Proposed Approach	88.56	92.42	90.44	90.35	86.52	88.39	87.47	93.26	90.27	91.54	94.96	93.21

Baseline 4: In this method, posts and comments are considered to evaluate the significance of emotion-related and seed features without considering the embedding model.

Abulaish et al. (2019): This approach incorporated sentimental aspects, such as anxiety and doubtful terms from the social media posts, and the embedding model for detecting rumors.

Ajao et al. (2019): This approach considered the relationship of rumors with the sentiments of the social media posts. It used the ratio of negative and positive emotions for the detection of sentiment-aware misinformation.

The experiments of the baselines and state-of-the-art approaches are performed to compare them with the proposed approach. The reasons for choosing these four classifiers are to follow the state-of-the-art approaches and exhibit the robustness of the extracted features. The performance of the classical machine learning algorithms is comparable to the *MLP* with one hidden layer, which signifies the robustness of the extracted features. The summarization of comparative results in terms of evaluation metrics, i.e., *Precision (P), Recall (R)*, and *F1-score (F1)*, are presented in Table 2. The proposed approach results show that the performance is significantly better for all four classification algorithms.

The best result of the proposed approach is obtained for the *MLP* classifier for all evaluation metrics. The outperformance of the proposed approach with one of the state-of-the-art methods (Ajao et al., 2019) ranges from $4.5 - 6.0\%$. The proposed approach remarkably outperformed (Abulaish et al., 2019) over all the classification algorithms. It shows that the features in the proposed approach are more versatile and broadened than (Abulaish et al., 2019), leading to a significant improvement in the performance. Moreover, baseline 3, considered only the emotion-related features for posts and comments, outperformed the state-of-the-art approach (Ajao et al., 2019) range from $2.1 - 2.7\%$ for the *SVM* and *GB* classification algorithms. It can also be observed from Table 2 that when the feature size is large, *MLP* performs better, while in baseline 4, where the feature size is small, *GB* performs better.

The experiments demonstrate the significant improvement of the detection task when combining emotion-related features with a embedding model. The performance analysis of the baselines also demonstrates that consideration of the emotions in comments improved the weight of the feature vectors and enhanced the performance significantly. The outperformance of the proposed approach and remarkable improvement against the baselines and state-of-the-art methods signifies that incorporating emotion-related features with psycholinguistic features enhances the rumor detection task.

5 Conclusion and Future Work

In this paper, we have presented an emotion-enhanced and psycholinguistic features-based approach for rumor detection that makes use of various emotion-related and linguistic features extracted from posts and comments. The embedding model is used to learn emotion-related semantic information from the posts and comments. The experimental results reveal a significant correlation between rumors and emotions, and demonstrate that emotion-related features substantially enhance rumor detection tasks, and are effective when combined with psycholinguistic features and an embedding model. It can also be concluded that utilizing the underlying features of comments improves the performance of the rumor detection task. The proposed approach can be extended to improve the extraction of emotion-related features that are not explicitly mentioned in the posts and comments. It can also be expanded to take into account the emotions that are embedded in image captions and multimedia.

References

Muhammad Abulaish, Nikita Kumari, Mohd Fazil, and Basanta Singh. 2019. A graph-theoretic embedding-based approach for rumor detection in twitter. In *Proceedings of the 18th IEEE/WIC/ACM International Conference on Web Intelligence, Thessaloniki, Greece*, pages 466–470. Association for Computing Machinery.

Oluwaseun Ajao, Deepayan Bhowmik, and Shahrzad Zargari. 2019. Sentiment aware fake news detection on online social networks. In *Proceedings of the 44th IEEE International Conference on Acoustics, Speech and Signal Processing (ICASSP), Brighton, UK*, pages 2507–2511. IEEE.

Anjali Bhardwaj and Muhammad Abulaish. 2023. MINDS: A multi-label emotion and sentiment classification dataset related to covid-19. In *Proceedings of The First Workshop on Context-aware NLP in eHealth (WNLPe-Health 2022) co-located with The nineteenth International Conference on Natural Language Processing (ICON-2022), Delhi, India, December 15-18, 2022.*

David B Buller and Judee K Burgoon. 1996. Interpersonal deception theory. *Communication theory*, 6(3):203–242.

Maria Mercedes Ferreira Caceres, Juan Pablo Sosa, Jannel A Lawrence, Cristina Sestacovschi, Atiyah Tidd-Johnson, Muhammad Haseeb UI Rasool, Vinay Kumar Gadamidi, Saleha Ozair, Krunal Pandav, Claudia Cuevas-Lou, et al. 2022. The impact of misinformation on the covid-19 pandemic. *AIMS public health*, 9(2):262.

Arjun Choudhry, Inder Khatri, Minni Jain, and Dinesh Kumar Vishwakarma. 2022. An emotion-aware multitask approach to fake news and rumor detection using transfer learning. *IEEE Transactions on Computational Social Systems*, pages 1–12.

Diwen Dong, Fuqiang Lin, Guowei Li, and Bo Liu. 2022. Sentiment-aware fake news detection on social media with hypergraph attention networks. In *2022 IEEE International Conference on Systems, Man, and Cybernetics (SMC)*, pages 2174–2180. IEEE.

Paul Ekman. 1992. An argument for basic emotions. *Cognition & emotion*, 6(3-4):169–200.

Bilal Ghanem, Paolo Rosso, and Francisco Rangel. 2020. An emotional analysis of false information in social media and news articles. *ACM Trans. Internet Technol.*, 20(2).

Anastasia Giachanou, Paolo Rosso, and Fabio Crestani. 2019. Leveraging emotional signals for credibility detection. In *Proceedings of the 42nd International ACM SIGIR Conference on Research and Development in Information Retrieval*, SIGIR'19, page 877–880, New York, NY, USA. Association for Computing Machinery.

Anastasia Giachanou, Paolo Rosso, Ida Mele, and Fabio Crestani. 2018. Emotional influence prediction of news posts. In *Proceedings of the International AAAI Conference on Web and Social Media*, volume 12.

Vipin Gupta, Rina Kumari, Nischal Ashok, Tirthankar Ghosal, and Asif Ekbal. 2022. MMM: An emotion and novelty-aware approach for multilingual multimodal misinformation detection. In *Findings of the Association for Computational Linguistics: AACL-IJCNLP 2022*, pages 464–477, Online only. Association for Computational Linguistics.

Asimul Haque and Muhammad Abulaish. 2022. A graph-based approach leveraging posts and reactions for detecting rumors on online social media. In *Proceedings of the 36th Pacific Asia Conference on Language, Information and Computation*, pages 533–544, Manila, Philippines. De La Salle University.

Clayton Hutto and Eric Gilbert. 2014. VADER: A parsimonious rule-based model for sentiment analysis of social media text. In *Proceedings of the international AAAI conference on web and social media*, volume 8, pages 216–225.

Jumayel Islam, Lu Xiao, and Robert E. Mercer. 2020. A lexicon-based approach for detecting hedges in informal text. In *Proceedings of the Twelfth Language Resources and Evaluation Conference*, pages 3109–3113, Marseille, France. European Language Resources Association.

Elena Kochkina, Maria Liakata, and Arkaitz Zubiaga. 2018. All-in-one: Multi-task learning for rumour verification. In *Proceedings of the 27th International Conference on Computational Linguistics*, Santa Fe, New Mexico, USA. Association for Computational Linguistics.

Rina Kumari, Nischal Ashok, Tirthankar Ghosal, and Asif Ekbal. 2021. A multitask learning approach for fake news detection: Novelty, emotion, and sentiment lend a helping hand. In *2021 International Joint Conference on Neural Networks (IJCNN)*, pages 1–8.

A Mackey, Susan Gauch, and Kevin Labille. 2021. Detecting fake news through emotion analysis. In *Proceedings of the 13th International Conference on Information, Process, and Knowledge Management*, pages 65–71.

Cameron Martel, Gordon Pennycook, and David G Rand. 2020. Reliance on emotion promotes belief in fake news. *Cognitive research: principles and implications*, 5:1–20.

Saif Mohammad. 2018. Word affect intensities. In *Proceedings of the Eleventh International Conference on Language Resources and Evaluation (LREC 2018)*, Miyazaki, Japan. European Language Resources Association (ELRA).

Saif M. Mohammad and Peter D. Turney. 2013. Crowdsourcing a word-emotion association lexicon. *Computational Intelligence*, 29(3):436–465.

Myle Ott, Yejin Choi, Claire Cardie, and Jeffrey T. Hancock. 2011. Finding deceptive opinion spam by any stretch of the imagination. In *Proceedings of the 49th Annual Meeting of the Association for Computational Linguistics: Human Language Technologies*, pages 309–319, Portland, Oregon, USA. Association for Computational Linguistics.

Bo Pang, Lillian Lee, et al. 2008. Opinion mining and sentiment analysis. *Foundations and Trends® in information retrieval*, 2(1–2):1–135.

James W Pennebaker, Ryan L Boyd, Kayla Jordan, and Kate Blackburn. 2015. The development and psychometric properties of liwc2015. Technical report.

Jeffrey Pennington, Richard Socher, and Christopher D Manning. 2014. Glove: Global vectors for word representation. In *Proceedings of the 2014 conference on empirical methods in natural language processing (EMNLP)*, pages 1532–1543.

Rosalind W Picard. 2000. *Affective computing*. MIT press.

Robert Plutchik. 1982. A psychoevolutionary theory of emotions.

Robert Plutchik. 2001. The nature of emotions: Human emotions have deep evolutionary roots, a fact that may explain their complexity and provide tools for clinical practice. *American scientist*, 89(4):344–350.

Juan Manuel Pérez, Juan Carlos Giudici, and Franco Luque. 2021. pysentimiento: A python toolkit for sentiment analysis and socialnlp tasks.

Nicolas Pröllochs, Dominik Bär, and Stefan Feuerriegel. 2021. Emotions explain differences in the diffusion of true vs. false social media rumors. *Scientific Reports*, 11(1):22721.

Hannah Rashkin, Eunsol Choi, Jin Yea Jang, Svitlana Volkova, and Yejin Choi. 2017. Truth of varying shades: Analyzing language in fake news and political fact-checking. In *Proceedings of the 2017 Conference on Empirical Methods in Natural Language Processing*, pages 2931–2937, Copenhagen, Denmark. Association for Computational Linguistics.

James A Russell. 2003. Core affect and the psychological construction of emotion. *Psychological review*, 110(1):145.

Tiberiu Sosea, Chau Pham, Alexander Tekle, Cornelia Caragea, and Junyi Jessy Li. 2022. Emotion analysis and detection during COVID-19. In *Proceedings of the Thirteenth Language Resources and Evaluation Conference*, pages 6938–6947, Marseille, France. European Language Resources Association.

Soroush Vosoughi, Deb Roy, and Sinan Aral. 2018. The spread of true and false news online. *Science*, 359(6380):1146–1151.

Nesar Ahmad Wasi and Muhammad Abulaish. 2020. Document-level sentiment analysis through incorporating prior domain knowledge into logistic regression. In *2020 IEEE/WIC/ACM International Joint Conference on Web Intelligence and Intelligent Agent Technology (WI-IAT)*, pages 969–974. IEEE.

Theresa Wilson, Janyce Wiebe, and Paul Hoffmann. 2005. Recognizing contextual polarity in phrase-level sentiment analysis. In *Proceedings of Human Language Technology Conference and Conference on Empirical Methods in Natural Language Processing*, pages 347–354, Vancouver, British Columbia, Canada. Association for Computational Linguistics.

Yang Xu, Jie Guo, Weidong Qiu, Zheng Huang, Enes Altuncu, and Shujun Li. 2022. " comments matter and the more the better!": Improving rumor detection with user comments. In *2022 IEEE International Conference on Trust, Security and Privacy in Computing and Communications (TrustCom)*, pages 383–390. IEEE.

Xinyi Zhou and Reza Zafarani. 2020. A survey of fake news: Fundamental theories, detection methods, and opportunities. *ACM Computing Surveys (CSUR)*, 53(5):1–40.

Arkaitz Zubiaga, Ahmet Aker, Kalina Bontcheva, Maria Liakata, and Rob Procter. 2018. Detection and resolution of rumours in social media: A survey. *ACM Computing Surveys (CSUR)*, 51(2):1–36.

The Future of Meat: Sentiment Analysis of Food Tweets

Matīss Rikters
National Institute of Advanced
Industrial Science and Technology
{name.surname}@aist.go.jp

Maija Kāle
Faculty of Computing,
University of Latvia
{name.surname}@lu.lv

Abstract

The future of food largely depends on the future of meat, considering multiple policy recommendations that urge for a decrease in meat consumption due to its impact on human health and environmental sustainability. In view of the 'meat vs alternative protein' playing its own part in the overall polarisation of societal discourse, we explored the dynamics of sentiment related to meat and meat consumption on Twitter over a ten year period. Twitter is one of the best sources for tracing various food-related utterances in different cultures and societies since the food there is widely documented and discussed in multiple formats. We accumulate the necessary contextual knowledge of group dynamics in relation to the topic of meat consumption that can be useful when aspects influencing individual food choices are examined. In this paper, we analyse social media content written in a morphological complex and less-resourced language – Latvian.

1 Introduction

Food choice and food consumption play an important role in public health, as well as impact environmental sustainability profoundly. Obesity, type 2 diabetes and cardiovascular diseases are just a few of the health problems acquired due to the nutritional specifics of contemporary consumers (Min et al., 2019). While the impact of food on personal health is an area discussed by food policy makers and nutritionists globally, another new discourse has emerged in relation to food consumption, namely, the impact on planetary health or levels of biodiversity, pollution and CO2 that influence and shape climate change, as well as the planet's ecosystems overall (Grivins et al., 2020). One third of global carbon dioxide emissions are assigned to food systems, where the largest contribution comes from agriculture and land-use activities (estimated 71% of the total emissions), while the food supply chain – transport, consumption, retail and other related processes account for 29% respectively (Crippa et al., 2021). Meat production makes the largest impact when it comes to producing greenhouse gases, as it accounts for nearly 60% of all greenhouse gases from food production (Xu et al., 2021). Beef accounts for one quarter of the total emissions, and in general, the use of animals for meat causes twice the pollution of producing plant-based foods (Xu et al., 2021).

High emissions that meat production causes in the context of climate change have led to the current food start-up and innovation scene being dominated by ideas that focus on developing alternative plant-based proteins. Thus, the discourse on the future of food to a considerable extent consists of the future of meat. Alternative proteins, lab-grown meat, vegan diets, and flexitarian lifestyles – all of these concepts contribute to the discussion on how or if we will be consuming meat in the future. Despite a rather uniform policy push towards reduced meat consumption (Lancet, 2018), the issue is growing more polarised on the level of social sentiment (Grivins et al., 2020), while increasing amounts of investments flow into meat replacement innovation. Currently, however, there are no signs of a mass shift away from meat consumption worldwide.

One of the best venues for tracing sentiment towards particular food consumption is social media where food is widely documented and discussed in multiple formats (Min et al., 2019). In comparison to other sources of analysis, social media data allows us to trace spontaneous reactions when people tweet without delay, thus avoiding potential biases which might have arisen using other opinion-gathering methods, e.g., surveys and food diaries (Laguna et al., 2020). Social network data analysis has reached popularity in consumer studies, where food language data and images are analysed. Food turns out to be one of the key themes discussed on Twitter, the social network that we focus on in

Proceedings of the 11th International Workshop on Natural Language Processing for Social Media, pages 38–46
November 1, 2023.

our work. As primarily a platform for text, not for images, and due to its accessibility for research purposes, Twitter is the digital space where it has become possible to follow the most random details of the everyday lives of tweeters – including the information on what, how and where they eat (Kāle et al., 2021).

We have chosen the Twitter social network for the analysis due to the availability of a large food-related data corpus in the Latvian language that was recently released – the Latvian Twitter Eater Corpus (LTEC (Sproģis and Rikters, 2020)). We focused on any entries concerning meat and meat products found in food-related tweets over a period of more than ten years. The tweet sentiment was then analysed in view of their positive, neutral or negative valence. Keeping in mind that social media are generally believed to showcase mostly positive experiences (Croijmans et al., 2020), we carried out a general sentiment analysis of the food tweets. We looked at the depiction of meat and meat products in temporal dynamics, thus trying to capture the historical as well as the contemporary 'Zeitgeist' in relation to meat consumption as it is depicted in the Latvian-speaking community. Besides an analysis of meat, we also looked into the depiction of vegan and vegetarian food on Twitter along with the debates about alternative proteins.

When analysing the discourse of meat in social media, it is important to be aware of the context the particular society is operating in. Regarding Latvian food culture and national cuisine general agreement is that the basis of Latvian cuisine is potato, dairy products, fish and meat, and pork in particular. It has formed as a heritage of peasant food in melange with aristocratic influence, similarly as in other European countries.[1] Somewhat better understanding of food consumption can be based on different seasons that Latvian society lives through during the year. As a Northern European country, Latvia has four distinct seasons where autumn and winter are relatively cold, dark and rainy, while summers are short and warm. What regards food choices, any society is sensitive to temperature and weather fluctuations, which is particularly evident in countries with greater seasonal variations in temperature (Spence, 2021). Latvia is a country with great seasonal variation in temperature, and thus, serves as good sandbox for weather related food data analysis. As previous research illustrates, Latvia also has its seasonal food preferences as depicted in social media: grey peas, tangerines and gingerbread during Christmas time, and cold soup strawberries and ice cream during hot spring and summer time (Kāle et al., 2021).

The driving motivation of this research has been to build a better understanding of the world, in particular looking into food consumption and food-related information sharing on social media. Food choices that consumers make affect public health and the planet's sustainability to a large extent, however, due to the interdisciplinary nature of food, many important topics have been under-researched in narrow scope research disciplines. This research aims to fill the gap and provide a methodology focused on sentiment analysis on how to understand food consumers given the role that social media play in modern lifestyles. With our approach, we aim to contribute to a growing research area that focuses on interdisciplinary research inquiries and insights into future of the food (Velasco et al., 2021). Collecting food-related data poses a yet unsolved challenge, thus, innovative ways to use social media and other large-scale data are the key innovative approach that this research offers.

2 Related Work

Food computing, a field that our research belongs to, is a novel, interdisciplinary, and future-oriented research area aiming to improve public health through a better understanding of food consumers. Empowered by new technology-based solutions, this interdisciplinary research area is expanding within the academic research that deals with food consumption, public health issues, and increasingly so – also within the environmental well-being of the planet. The term 'food computing' describes the use of computational methods when analysing different food-related data. The focus lies on large-scale data or 'big data' and the opportunities to collect the data in order to analyse food perception, recognition, and retrieval, as well as devise recommendations for prediction and monitoring. Food computing is an interdisciplinary field which in a broad sense encompasses food-related studies performed via computer science. In order to understand the rationale behind various food-related issues, food computing has grasped the opportunities opened through the web revolution: social networks, mobile networks, and the internet of things

[1] News portal of Latvian Radio and Latvian Television https://eng.lsm.lv/article/culture/food-drink/traditional-and-national-latvian-foods-whats-the-difference.a466155/

(IoT), which allow their users to easily share food images, recipes, cooking videos, or record food diaries, creating large-scale food data sets (Min et al., 2019). The rationale for food computing development has been an inquiry to design food recommendation systems. Such food recommendation systems, in turn, must understand users and their food choices in context. This research contributes to understanding this context.

There have been high expectations for the utility of large-scale data in food research, although a developed framework for its applicability is still lacking. Large-scale data or 'big data' are typically referred to large amounts of data produced very quickly by a high number of diverse sources. Other definitions related to big data highlight their unprecedented scale (volume), fragmentation (high variety), and real-time increase (velocity). While the use of big data is under increasing academic scrutiny, the field holds vast potential for opening new research areas in terms of food-related studies. Thus, for example, the term 'big data' is seldom used in relation to food safety, mainly because food safety data and information are scattered across the food, health, and agriculture sectors (Marvin et al., 2017).

The interdisciplinary characteristic of food-related data is also an issue in consumer research when it comes to utilising social network data. There are limitations concerning the fragmented nature of social media data: for example, Twitter users are digitally active and a relatively wealthy part of the population, thus, the results cannot be generalised by referring to the whole society. Nevertheless, even acknowledging the fragmentation, new research inquiries in using social media data can be of value for policymakers and those nudging particular behaviours among food consumers (Kāle and Rikters, 2021). Another research direction that proves the utility of social media analysis is looking at how digital food affects our analogue lives and eating behaviour in particular (Andersen et al., 2021). Correlating social media results related to food in a particular region with the sales data could be the next step in our analytical approach, as there is a common agreement that digital content impacts purchasing behaviours in our analogue lives, however, this lacks granularity when it comes to exact correlations and proof of statements.

As the research illustrates, food is bound by culture and climate, and the language employed in tweets within a geographic region reveals certain specifics that should be taken into account (Metcalfe, 2019). By analysing the frequency rates of food-related tweets, it has been possible to detect seasonality as well as to identify certain cultural aspects related to traditional Latvian cuisine. It has also revealed food-related tweeting activity in relation to particular days of the week and particular times of the day, uncovering the tweeting activity concerning specific foods during specific times of the day (Kāle et al., 2021). Knowledge and higher levels of precision about certain foods that are susceptible to seasonality peaks can help policymakers to shape their stories that will resonate on social media and lead to better public health through more healthy food choices. Meanwhile, the very same knowledge can also be used by food marketers who do not necessarily promote the most healthy food options for consumers (Velasco et al., 2021).

A deeper understanding of language and how we describe foods is, however, a prerequisite to understanding the dynamics between the individual and the group when it comes to food choice. One of the most notable domains where individual and group behaviour can be traced via language is the domain of healthy vs tasty food. One of the most recognised challenges that hinder food consumers from choosing healthier food options is the strong tension between tastiness and healthiness that plays a decisive role in food choice and is important for obesity and other diseases, as well as environmental consciousness. This tension has been labelled as untasty = healthy intuition (Mai and Hoffmann, 2015). This tension is well seen in language differences in how people talk about comfort foods versus healthy foods, where comfort foods are described sensually – e.g. 'broad-shouldered wine' or 'sexy dessert' (Jurafsky, 2014), while healthy foods are depicted as rational, pragmatic and easy to cook items (Kāle and Agbozo, 2020). In particular, to the language of meat or vegetarian dishes as its opposite, there is a growing field of research looking into the language used for describing meat dishes versus vegan and vegetarian dishes. The same conclusions remain: the language of how the dish is described matters, and the taste of the dish can change just because the wording of how food is described, has been changed (Bacon et al., 2019). Instead of language analysis of how particular foods are described, we focus on sentiment analysis which can be of great use for food language analysts to gain a more holistic view of how particular foods are discussed in different societies.

Finally, we aim to illustrate the utility of data coming from languages less resourced and less spoken. Thus, the Latvian Twitter Eater Corpus (LTEC), a unique resource devised for the analysis of Latvian food-related tweets, has been used in this research. It might serve as a pilot corpus for other less-resourced languages and contribute to a better understanding of the differences in food narratives depending on the language we use (Fenko et al., 2010).

3 Methodology and Experiment Setup

Our analysis is based on inspecting the Latvian Twitter Eater Corpus (LTEC (Sproģis and Rikters, 2020)), which contains 2.4M tweets generated by 169k users collected for over 10 years by following 363 eating-related keywords in Latvian. The dataset provides some additional metadata about each tweet, such as location (when available), all food items mentioned in the tweet text, and a separate subset of tweets with manually annotated sentiment classes – positive, neutral and negative.

Since the corpus contains normalised versions of all food items in singular nominative form for each tweet, we used these to further select only the specific tweets for our analysis. This was done by firstly compiling a list of most used meat-related nouns (see Table 1), and then selecting only the very narrow subset which mentions either beef, chicken or pork.

3.1 Sentiment Analysis

We used the 5420 annotated tweets to fine-tune a pre-trained multilingual BERT (Devlin et al., 2019) model for the sentiment analysis task along with ~20,000 sentiment-annotated Latvian tweets from other sources[2] so that the model would generalise better. We evaluated the sentiment model on the 743 tweet test set provided in LTEC and reached an accuracy of 74.06%. Our result outperforms the best accuracy reported by the authors of LTEC, who used a Naive Bayes model on stemmed data and reached 61.23%. However, this was expected since they used ~20% less training data, and BERT or other transformer-based models have outperformed previous state-of-the-art methods in many language processing tasks, including classification. We then used the model to automatically classify all tweets in LTEC as positive, neutral or negative for further analysis.

3.2 Human Evaluation

To verify the quality of the sentiment analysis model, we selected 50 random automatically classified tweets from each year between 2011 and 2020 and performed a manual evaluation. Twelve human evaluators were asked to individually judge each of the 500 predictions by the model and provide a suggested alternative sentiment class for cases where they deemed the model to be incorrect. We used the majority vote of the human evaluators as the correct answer in cases where they disagreed on a particular evaluation and considered two classifications as correct in the 21 cases where the majority opinion was split in half (for example, 6 positive and 6 neutral). The overall agreement of the evaluators was 70.48% with a free marginal kappa (Randolph, 2005) of 0.56 (values from 0.40 to 0.75 are considered intermediate to good agreement).

The accuracy of the model according to the majority of human evaluators on this set was even higher, reaching 86.40%, while the accuracy of the average human evaluator compared to the majority was only 80.25%. This shows that 1) the tweet texts are not always trivial enough to be unequivocally classified into just one of the three sentiment classes, and 2) the model is good enough to be used on the scale of the whole dataset.

3.3 Limitations and Assumptions

Our work has several important limitations that can be grouped into categories of 1) data availability, 2) tweet author's demographic profile, and 3) generalisation of the results. First, we cannot provide a specific demographic outlook of the usual tweet author from LTEC, and our analysis includes tweets by general digitally literate people active on Twitter. Second, while our sentiment analysis model is fairly accurate, misclassifications may still occur, especially in longer, multi-sentence tweets. Therefore, we use the automatically assigned sentiment classes only as an overview of the trend, but not for fine-grained analysis of specific tweets. Third, considering the limitations discussed, our results are not an exact extrapolation of meat-related food perception in Latvian society. Nevertheless, our approach utilises the growing LTEC and adds to

[2] https://github.com/Usprogis/Latvian-Twitter-Eater-Corpus/tree/master/sub-corpora/sentiment-analysis#other-latvian-twitter-sentiment-corpora

liver	sausage	chop	bacon
deer	bratwurst	ham	**beef**
steak	**pork**	cutlet	steak
meatball	turkey	ribs	goose
chicken	fillet	meat	salami
roast	schnitzel	lamb	gyros

Table 1: Meat products included in our experiment.

the understanding of the impact of meat on the part of the Latvian society, which tweets about food.

4 Experiment Results

Before turning to the sentiment analysis results regarding meat-related tweets, we first look at how sentiment is distributed in all food tweets of the dataset. In tweets from 2011-2020, we can observe an overall decrease in positive sentiment and a rise in negative sentiment, as well as a comparatively large share of neutral tweets. Figure 1 shows the overall sentiment distribution of that period. It is also visible that the number of positive tweets was decreasing until 2015, from 2015 onward there has been an increase in neutral tweets, and from around 2018 the amount of negative tweets has been increasing.

4.1 Meat-related

Figure 2 shows sentiment over time of meat-related tweets all together. Aside from selecting all inflections of the word "meat", we also include the specific meat products listed in Table 1 in this overview. Here we can see that up to 2016 Twitter users were not overly active in discussions around meat overall. The share of neutral sentiment tweets has significantly grown between 2016 and 2018 and has remained mostly stable since then, while the amount of more polarising opinions – positive and negative meat-related tweets seems to be still growing ever so slightly. Even though between 2011 and 2017 the level of negative tweets is mostly flat, the one spike in March of 2013 can be attributed to a scandal over the alleged use of horse meat in a popular butcher chain from Latvia[3]. Since 2016 tweets with negative sentiment have surpassed the positive ones, although the bulk of the meat-related food tweets can still be classified as neutral.

To have a more detailed look into specific meat products, Figure 3 illustrates the differences in sentiment related to chicken, beef and pork. Again, we can see a sharp rise in neutral tweets starting from 2016, which could be explained by the increase in popularity of publicly available lunch offers at local eateries and other types of food-specific advertising. A neutral tweet in this case is a tweet that simply informs about the daily offer at a cafe or restaurant without any emotional connotations to the food listed on those offers. With the onset of the Covid-19 pandemic, however, neutrality has given way to either positive or negative valence instead. One possible reason for this could be due to the closure of restaurants and other public spaces for food consumption, and accordingly less such neutral lunch-offer type tweets from the corporate sector players.

4.2 Vegans, Vegetarians and Alternative Proteins

In addition to posts directly mentioning meat-related products, we were also interested in exploring if any mentions of meat alternatives are mentioned and how they are perceived on Twitter. Figures 4 and 5 give an overview of tweets mentioning either 'vegan' or 'vegetarian' in any inflection in the Latvian language or any inflection of the word 'protein' in Latvian. We can observe overall lower amounts of tweets when compared to ones mentioning 'meat', as well as a higher tendency of positive sentiment tweets. The dominance of positive sentiment tweets over neutral tweets that dominate meat-related discourses can signify that there are few tweets by e.g. corporate sector in a form of lunch offers or sales of vegan/vegetarian food or any other marketing-related neutral tweets. Instead, veganism and vegetarianism as not yet a mainstream discourses are mostly discussed by people with strictly positive or negative attitudes towards them. Regarding negative sentiments, it should be noted that 'vegan' sometimes is used as a swearword in Latvian Twitter space, referring to a person that is weak, incapable of activities requiring physical strength and has not had job experience as belongs to younger generations. A new term 'soy latte drinkers' appeared during the debate when mandatory military service was renewed due to Russia's invasion of Ukraine. Young people who protested the mandatory military service were ironically called 'soy latte drinkers', implying their physical weakness due to vegetarian or vegan lifestyles. This signifies that social media sentiment

[3]https://www.theguardian.com/uk-news/2013/jul/19/horsemeat-scandal-meat-pies-latvia

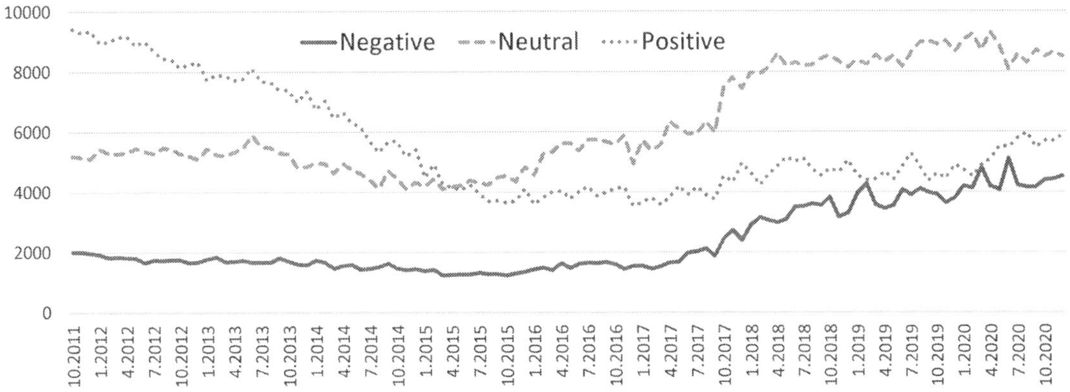

Figure 1: Distribution of overall tweet sentiment in LTEC over time from 2011 to 2020.

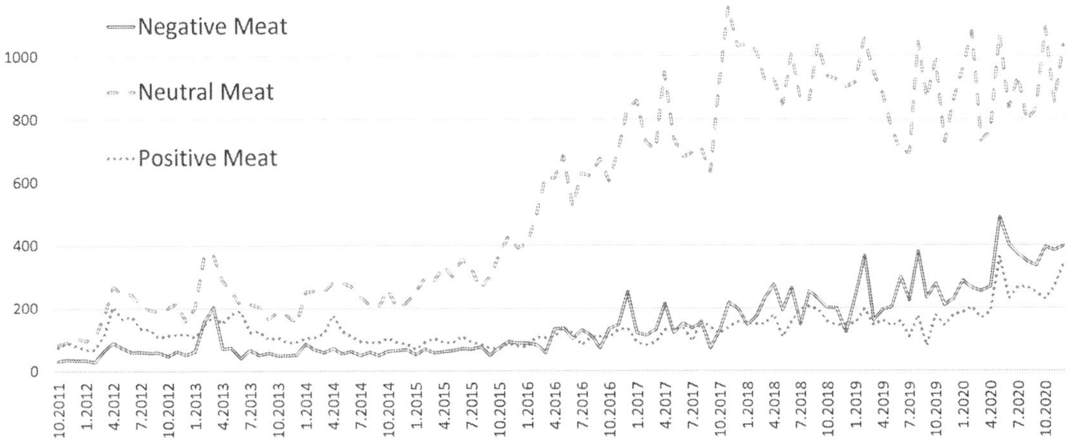

Figure 2: Temporal sentiment dynamics of meat-related tweets LTEC in 2011-2020.

analysis has also potential to reveal stereotypes existing in the particular societies in relation to food and health, and potentially serve as a litmus test for fake news spread in relation to lifestyles, health and food.

With regard to proteins, we see similar dynamics as to the vegan and vegetarian discourse, albeit with even fewer frequencies, which means that discussion on proteins in Latvian Twitter space is very low, and if it takes place, then it is mostly positive or neutral, with little generated, informative content. These results of low levels of frequencies signify that vegan, and vegetarian diets and the quest for alternative proteins remain marginal in everyday discussions of Twitter users in Latvia.

5 Conclusion

We started with a statement that the future of food will to a large extent be determined/dependent on the future of meat since policy recommendations urge for decreased meat consumption. This has paved the way for e.g. alternative protein development as more and more investments flow into this area, as well as vegetarian/vegan diet appreciation, which has come to shape the discourse in a stark conflict with the discourse of meat lovers. Social media in this case can serve as a litmus test for the public mood and attitudes towards meat consumption. Our research reveals that negative sentiment about meat on Latvian Twitter is steadily rising, although the neutral mood is still holding its fair share of dominance. The spread of the Covid-19 pandemic seems to have notably decreased neutrality towards certain meat types – chicken, beef and pork. All these data help us to trace the public attitude towards meat consumption and assess its readiness for change towards the future of less meat consumption as envisioned by policymakers. Looking at the sentiments and frequencies regarding vegan/vegetarian food and protein related, we con-

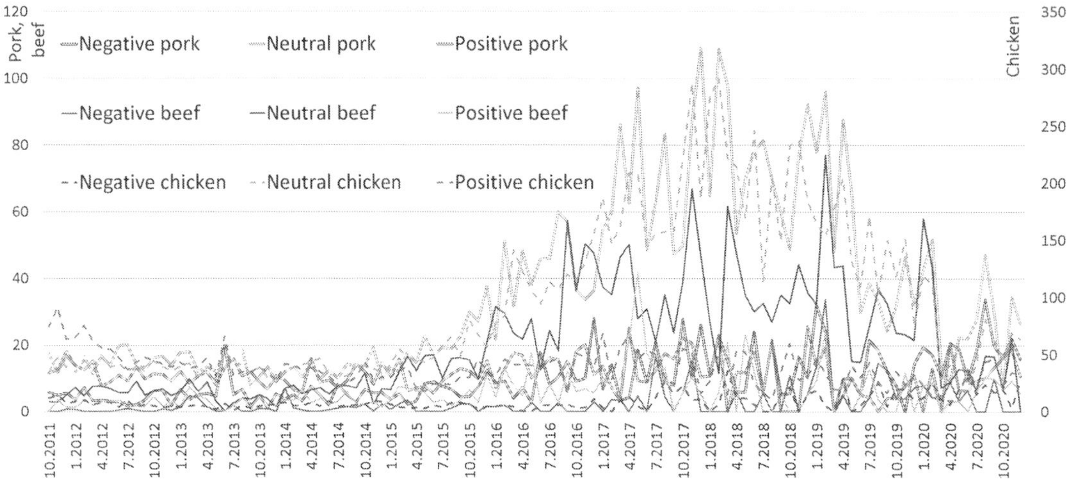

Figure 3: Temporal sentiment dynamics in 2011-2020: tweets mentioning beef, chicken or pork.

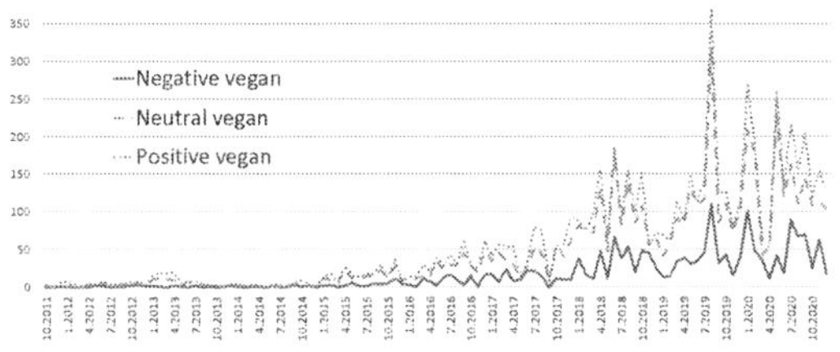

Figure 4: Distribution of tweet sentiment in LTEC over time from 2011 to 2020 of tweets mentioning vegan or vegetarian.

clude that there are not many discussions related to these themes on Twitter when compared to meat, especially in comparison to neutral, informative tweets about meat.

These data can be useful for policymakers working with the public diets' shift towards more environmentally conscious choices. Knowing the dominating discourse in the society related to meat and being able to trace the sentiment changes over time, can potentially best signify the society's maturity for change as suggested by public health policymakers. These data can be useful also for industry players, such as retailers and meat producers who shape their own discourse on meat consumption in particular markets. For marketers, temporal sentiment dynamics related to meat are valuable sales and marketing data and can be utilised in their promotional activities.

Taking into account the seldom use of social media data in academic research due to the fragmented nature – user demographics unknown, data only from the relatively wealthy and digitally active part of society, particular preferences of the social network in focus – Twitter, while other different social networks also of use, we consider that our research provides important encouragement to utilise social network data. The utility of our research results can be seen via creating valuable insights into group dynamics of the particular society, and while fragmented and in many ways incomplete, social media data of a particular social network Twitter, can to a large extent impact individual food choices. Group dynamics of social media can signify and determine the trends that impact individual preferences and ultimately food choices. Therefore, when developing individual food and health apps, it is of utmost importance to include the context data of the individual, society, national cuisine, weather and seasonality in their analysis. Social media data serve to signify those various influential context factors as can be seen also from our analysis of a particular focus on meat consumption sentiments in the Latvian Twitter community.

In future work we aim to refine our sentiment analysis approach – sometimes it was difficult to determine if the sentiment was positive or negative, especially if the tweet was ironic. Including more gradations of sentiments could be useful for us to trace the direction of morals when it comes to meat consumption. It could also allow us to separate better tweets, where 'vegan' or 'soy latte drinker' were used as allegories rather than food choices. This leads us to the necessity to collaborate with anthropologists and food historians on how food is used as an allegory to describe other processes in society instead of purely food perception and food

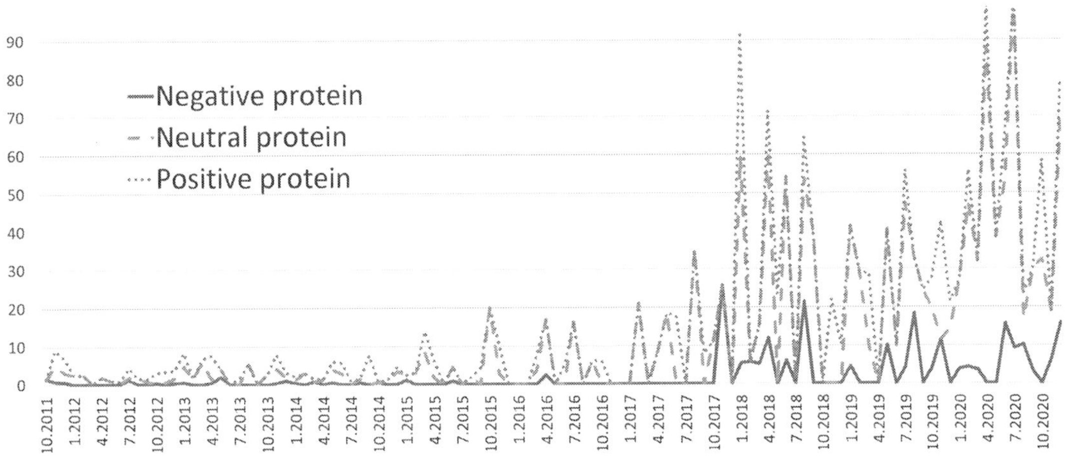

Figure 5: Distribution of tweet sentiment in LTEC over time from 2011 to 2020 of tweets mentioning protein.

choices from a dietary perspective. Furthermore, these data also invite for cross-checking spread of stereotypes and fake news related to food consumption and health aspects. This can be crucial for any public health policy strategic development – to know what kind of stereotypes and prejudices exist in certain groups, and how they are spread in social media.

As illustrated earlier, Latvia provides a good case of food-related tweet sentiment analysis due to its four seasons and rather different temperatures throughout the year. In the future, we aim to correlate the food sentiment data with the weather data to determine the impact that the weather has on our food choices. We also plan to carry out weather impact analysis on meat choices in particular.

We plan to release the additional data and models generated in this research publicly. The automatically assigned sentiment classes will be added to the main corpus data repository on GitHub[4], and publish the sentiment analysis model to Hugging Face's model hub[5].

Limitations

In this work, we only considered training our models on data that is publicly available to enable reproducibility. Also, since hyper-parameter tuning on training large models is computationally very costly, we opt for choosing mostly default parameters in our experiments.

We would further like to note that Twitter is a platform and resource for the relatively affluent and digitally well connected members of society. Thus, the population which is most vulnerable and most sensitive to food price fluctuations remain outside the scope of this analysis.

Ethics Statement

Our work fully complies with the ACL Code of Ethics[6]. We use only publicly available datasets and relatively low compute amounts while conducting our experiments to enable reproducibility. All human data annotators were fairly compensated in accordance with market rates.

References

Tjark Andersen, Derek Byrne, and Qian Wang. 2021. How digital food affects our analog lives: The impact of food photography on healthy eating behavior. *Frontiers in Psychology*, 12:634261.

Linda Bacon, Jonathan Sands Wise, Sophie Attwood, and Daniel Vennard. 2019. The language of sustainable diets: A field study exploring the impact of renaming vegetarian dishes on u.k. café menus. In *World Resources Institute*.

Monica Crippa, Efisio Solazzo, D. Guizzardi, Fabio Monforti, Francesco Tubiello, and Adrian Leip. 2021. Food systems are responsible for a third of global anthropogenic ghg emissions. *Nature Food*, 2:1–12.

Ilja Croijmans, Iris Hendrickx, Els Lefever, Asifa Majid, and Antal Van Den Bosch. 2020. Uncovering the language of wine experts. *Natural Language Engineering*, 26(5):511–530.

Jacob Devlin, Ming-Wei Chang, Kenton Lee, and Kristina Toutanova. 2019. BERT: Pre-training of

[4]https://github.com/Usprogis/Latvian-Twitter-Eater-Corpus/

[5]https://huggingface.co/models

[6]https://www.aclweb.org/portal/content/acl-code-ethics

deep bidirectional transformers for language understanding. In *Proceedings of the 2019 Conference of the North American Chapter of the Association for Computational Linguistics: Human Language Technologies, Volume 1 (Long and Short Papers)*, pages 4171–4186, Minneapolis, Minnesota. Association for Computational Linguistics.

Anna Fenko, Jacco J. Otten, and Hendrik N. J. Schifferstein. 2010. Describing product experience in different languages: The role of sensory modalities. *Fuel and Energy Abstracts*.

Mikelis Grivins, Afton Halloran, and Maija Kāle. 2020. *Eight megatrends in Nordic-Baltic food systems*. Nordisk Ministerråd.

Daniel Jurafsky. 2014. *The Language of Food: A Linguist Reads the Menu*. W. W. Norton, New York, New York, United States.

Maija Kāle and Ebenezer Agbozo. 2020. Tracing complexity in food blogging entries. *CEUR Workshop Proceedings*, abs/2007.05552.

Maija Kāle and Matīss Rikters. 2021. Fragmented and valuable: Following sentiment changes in food tweets. *Smell, Taste, and Temperature Interfaces CHI 2021 workshop*, abs/2106.04903.

Maija Kāle, Jurģis Šķilters, and Matīss Rikters. 2021. Tracing multisensory food experiences on twitter. *International Journal of Food Design*, 6:181–212.

Laura Laguna, Susana Fiszman, Patricia Puerta, C Chaya, and Amparo Tárrega. 2020. The impact of covid-19 lockdown on food priorities. results from a preliminary study using social media and an online survey with spanish consumers. *Food Quality and Preference*, 86:104028.

The Lancet. 2018. We need to talk about meat. *The Lancet*, 392(10161):2237. Publisher: Elsevier.

Robert Mai and Stefan Hoffmann. 2015. How to combat the unhealthy = tasty intuition: The influencing role of health consciousness. *Journal of Public Policy & Marketing*, 34(1):63–83.

Hans J. P. Marvin, Esmée M. Janssen, Yamine Bouzembrak, Peter J. M. Hendriksen, and Martijn Staats. 2017. Big data in food safety: An overview. *Critical Reviews in Food Science and Nutrition*, 57(11):2286–2295. PMID: 27819478.

Robyn Metcalfe. 2019. *Food Routes: Growing Bananas in Iceland and Other Tales from the Logistics of Eating*. MIT Press, London, England.

Weiqing Min, Shuqiang Jiang, Linhu Liu, Yong Rui, and Ramesh Jain. 2019. A survey on food computing. *ACM Computing Surveys*, 52(5):1–36.

Justus J Randolph. 2005. Free-marginal multirater kappa (multirater k [free]): An alternative to fleiss' fixed-marginal multirater kappa. *Online submission*.

Charles Spence. 2021. Explaining seasonal patterns of food consumption. *International Journal of Gastronomy and Food Science*, 24:100332.

Uga Sproģis and Matīss Rikters. 2020. What Can We Learn From Almost a Decade of Food Tweets. In *In Proceedings of the 9th Conference Human Language Technologies - The Baltic Perspective (Baltic HLT 2020)*, volume 328, pages 191 – 198, Kaunas, Lithuania. IOS Press.

Carlos Velasco, Charles Michel, and Charles Spence. 2021. Gastrophysics: Current approaches and future directions. *International Journal of Food Design*, 6:137–152.

Xiaoming Xu, Prateek Sharma, Shijie Shu, Tzu-Shun Lin, Philippe Ciais, Francesco N Tubiello, Pete Smith, Nelson Campbell, and Atul K Jain. 2021. Global greenhouse gas emissions from animal-based foods are twice those of plant-based foods. *Nature Food*, 2(9):724–732.

Boosting Adverse Drug Event Normalization on Social Media: General-Purpose Model Initialization and Biomedical Semantic Text Similarity Benefit Zero-Shot Linking in Informal Contexts

François REMY
University of Ghent
francois.remy
@ugent.be

Simone Scaboro
University of Udine
scaboro.simone
@spes.uniud.it

Beatrice Portelli
University of Udine
portelli.beatrice
@spes.uniud.it

Abstract

Biomedical entity linking, also known as biomedical concept normalization, has recently witnessed the rise to prominence of zero-shot contrastive models. However, the pre-training material used for these models has, until now, largely consisted of specialist biomedical content such as MIMIC-III clinical notes (Johnson et al., 2016) and PubMed papers (Sayers et al., 2021; Gao et al., 2020). While the resulting in-domain models have shown promising results for many biomedical tasks, adverse drug event normalization on social media texts has so far remained challenging for them (Portelli et al., 2022). In this paper, we propose a new approach for adverse drug event normalization on social media relying on general-purpose model initialization via BioLORD (Remy et al., 2022) and a semantic-text-similarity fine-tuning named STS. Our experimental results on several social media datasets demonstrate the effectiveness of our proposed approach, by achieving state-of-the-art performance. Based on its strong performance across all the tested datasets, we believe this work could emerge as a turning point for the task of adverse drug event normalization on social media and has the potential to serve as a benchmark for future research in the field.

1 Introduction

Adverse drug events (ADEs) are unexpected and possibly undocumented negative effects related to the correct use of a drug, and they have the potential to result in serious harm to patients. ADEs can also increase hospitalization costs, reduce patient satisfaction, and erode trust in the health care system. For these reasons, ADEs are a major concern for patients, healthcare providers, and regulators.

However, detecting and reporting emerging ADEs (a process known as pharmacovigilance) is not an easy task (Pappa and Stergioulas, 2019). Most of the information about ADEs is buried in

Figure 1: Normalization of concepts in the clinical domain made large progresses, but social media content remains more challenging due to informal language.

unstructured text sources, such as medical case reports, social media posts, or online reviews (Audeh et al., 2020). The two latter sources often contain informal language, abbreviations, slang, or misspellings, that make machine learning models unable to accurately extract and normalize ADEs present within them, a process known as biomedical concept normalization. Models trained exclusively on clinical data are particularly likely to be affected (see Figure 1). This is a real concern, as mapping ADEs to standardized ontologies, such as MedDRA (Brown et al., 1999) or SNOMED CT (IHTSDO, 2008), is an important step to facilitate the analysis and comparison of ADE data across different sources and domains (Adel et al., 2019).

In a short time span, between the years 2020 and 2022, the field of biomedical concept normalization has seen significant advancements with the introduction of self-supervised contrastive models. Originally introduced by Chen et al. (2020) for computer vision, these models are trained to produce identical latent representations for multiple views of a same concept, yet contrasted representations for each concept. In the biomedical domain, these views are usually constructed based on biomedical ontologies, by pairing canonical names of a concept with some of their known synonyms.

Proceedings of the 11th International Workshop on Natural Language Processing for Social Media, pages 47–52
November 1, 2023.

State of the art biomedical entity normalization is now dominated by models relying on this technique such as BioSyn (Sung et al., 2020), CODER (Yuan et al., 2022), and SapBERT (Liu et al., 2021). What makes these models extremely versatile is that it is possible to encode a new set of target concepts at inference time, which means that using the same model is possible irrespective of the target ontology, enabling smooth system updates.

2 Our contributions

2.1 General-Purpose Initialization

All models cited thus far were initialized from language models pre-trained on text from the biomedical domain, as this is thought to improve entity normalization performance somewhat in the clinical domain. In this paper, we propose a new approach for adverse drug event normalization on social media by employing BioLORD, a general-purpose model initialization approach pioneered by Remy et al. (2022). We hypothesize that its pre-training on general texts will help tremendously in understanding the informal language used on social media, while previous state of the art models struggled at that specific task, due to the domain shift between clinical and social media languages.

2.2 MedSTS Finetuning

In addition, after noticing that semantic-text-similarity finetuning helps achieving better performance, we improve this new approach even further by incorporating two distinct semantic-text-similarity (STS) fine-tuning phases to the training, both before and after the BioLORD pre-training. We release the improved BioLORD-STS model as part of this paper, and show that it achieves a performance far exceeding the current state-of-the-art.

3 Methodology

In this paper, we set out to show that general-purpose models fine-tuned on biomedical definitions perform better, for the task of ADE normalization in the social media, than state-of-the-art models trained exclusively on biomedical corpora.

Our hypothesis is based on the following observations derived from the extensive ablation studies performed in the BioLORD pre-training paper (Remy et al., 2022): applying the BioLORD pre-training strategy on a general-purpose model can help the model learn to generalize across different writing styles, including non-clinical ones that are rare in biomedical corpora; meanwhile, possessing a strong biomedical knowledge at initialization time did not appear essential to achieve good performance when using the BioLORD pre-training.

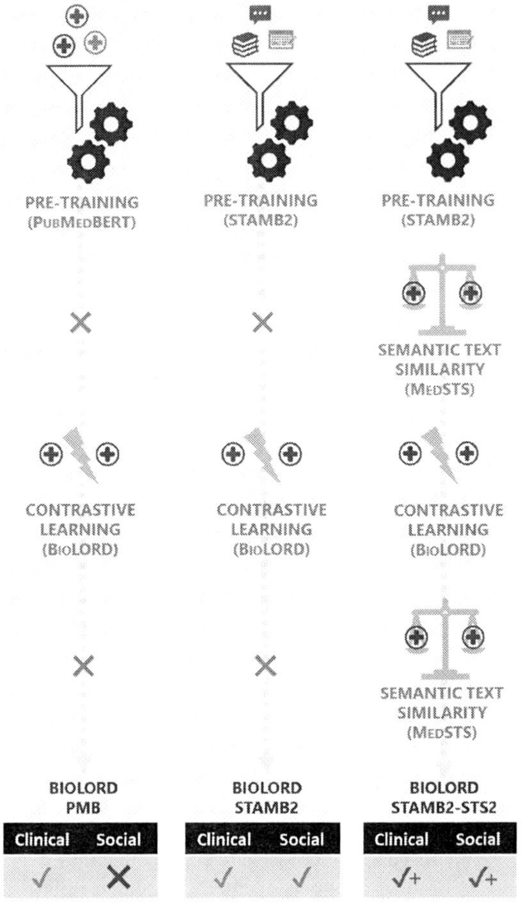

Figure 2: Schema of the pre-training and fine-tuning steps of the four candidate models: BioLORD-PMB, BioLORD-STAMB2, and BioLORD-STAMB2-STS2.

In a final experiment, we also verify that biomedical text similarity is a useful pre-training step to apply before training BioLORD-type models.

We benchmark all models on four social media datasets: CADEC (Karimi et al., 2015), PsyTAR (Zolnoori et al., 2019), SMM4H (Weissenbacher et al., 2019), and TwiMed (Alvaro et al., 2017), which are further described in Section 3.3.

Through this extensive benchmarking, we aim to demonstrate that our proposed approach significantly outperforms the previous state of the art in informal contexts, which cover a wide range of social media activities (such as: forum messages, online reviews, and tweets).

3.1 Candidate Models

To disentangle the impact of the base model initialization from the impact of the BioLORD pre-training strategy, we consider two different base models: STAMB2[1] (Reimers and Gurevych, 2019), the same general-purpose model used in the BioLORD paper, and PubMedBERT (Gu et al., 2020), a robust domain-specific model pre-trained on medical texts. The resulting models are named **BioLORD-STAMB2** and **BioLORD-PMB**.

We also analyze the effect of fine-tuning the models on a medical semantic text similarity task (STS) in addition to the BioLORD pre-training. We do so by fine-tuning some of the models on the MedSTS task (Wang et al., 2020), using the same hyperparameters described in the BioLORD paper. The base STAMB2 model is fine-tuned for STS before applying the BioLORD pre-training. This model then undergoes a second stage of STS fine-tuning, resulting in **BioLORD-STAMB2-STS2**.

Figure 2 illustrates the differences between the proposed models.

3.2 Baseline Models

We choose two BERT-based models trained with contrastive learning strategies as baselines: **CODER** (Yuan et al., 2022) and **SapBERT** (Liu et al., 2021). They are among the best dataset-agnostic models for medical term embeddings at the time of writing. Both of them are trained on the UMLS ontology (Bodenreider, 2004) and were tested on several term normalization datasets, showing promising results. SapBERT was the first large-scale contrastive model to leverage UMLS and is based on PubMedBERT. It is trained by using UMLS synonyms to create contrastive pairs. CODER, on the other hand, leverages both term-term pairs and term-relation-term triples.

3.3 Datasets

We evaluate all the candidate and baseline models using four medical entity normalization datasets containing ADEs. All of them contain informal texts coming from different social media platforms. One of the datasets also contains a subset of formal samples (TwiMed-PM). We include this subset in our experiments to verify that all the tested models perform well on ADE normalization in the clinical domain too.

[1]https://huggingface.co/sentence-transformers/all-mpnet-base-v2

The **TwiMed** dataset (Alvaro et al., 2017) provides a comparable corpus of texts from PubMed (abstracts) and Twitter (posts), allowing researchers in the area of pharmacovigilance to better understand the similarities and differences between the language used to describe disease and drug-related symptoms on PubMed (**TwiMed-PM**, clinical domain) and Twitter (**TwiMed-TW**, social media domain). Both sets of data contain 1000 samples.

The CSIRO Adverse Drug Event Corpus (**CADEC**) dataset (Karimi et al., 2015) is a corpus of user-generated reviews of drugs that has been annotated with adverse drug events (ADEs) and their normalization. It contains 1250 posts from a medical forum, which were annotated by a team of experts from the University of Arizona.

The Psychiatric Treatment Adverse Reactions (**PsyTAR**) dataset (Zolnoori et al., 2019) contains patients' expression of effectiveness and adverse drug events associated with psychiatric medications, originating from a sample of 891 drugs reviews posted by patients on an online healthcare forum.

The Social Media Mining for Health Applications (**SMM4H**) dataset (Gonzalez-Hernandez et al., 2020) is a dataset for Adverse Drug Event (ADE) normalization. It was used in the SMM4H 2020 shared task on ADE normalization. The aim of the subtask was to recognize ADE mentions from tweets and normalize them to their preferred term in the MedDRA ontology. The dataset includes 1212 tweets containing ADEs.

For each evaluated dataset, we perform zero-shot entity normalization using a setup identical to Portelli et al. (2022) with four test splits.

4 Results

We report the zero-shot evaluation results of the various models in Table 1.

Looking at the results on TwiMed-PM, the samples coming from the clinical domain, we observe that almost all of the models have a similar performance (between 69.99 and 70.60), showing that all models (general-purpose or in-domain) can reach a good performance on formal datasets.

The gap in performance of CODER and SapBERT between TwiMed-PM and all the social-media datasets highlights the existence of a significant difference in language distribution between texts in the clinical domain, and the less formal texts found in online reviews or social media.

	TwiMed-PM	CADEC	PsyTAR	SMM4H	TwiMed-TW
CODER	65.31 ± 1.85	35.29 ± 1.27	52.40 ± 0.71	33.14 ± 1.28	42.80 ± 2.06
SAPBERT	70.05 ± 1.56	40.42 ± 1.27	64.82 ± 1.36	43.37 ± 1.07	48.29 ± 2.85
BIOLORD-PMB	69.99 ± 1.87	58.23 ± 0.36	60.22 ± 0.84	41.80 ± 2.24	47.14 ± 2.21
BIOLORD-STAMB2	70.44 ± 1.19	58.69 ± 0.97	64.70 ± 0.76	46.51 ± 2.08	48.46 ± 1.53
BIOLORD-STAMB2-STS2	70.60 ± 1.19	60.28 ± 0.80	65.49 ± 0.74	47.33 ± 1.42	50.57 ± 1.72

Table 1: Accuracy@1 of the evaluated models on all the datasets. Datasets are ordered according to the formality of their language, from more formal (TwiMed-TW) to more informal (SMM4H and TwiMed-TW).

If we focus on the models trained using only the BioLORD pre-training, we can see that they perform better than the two state-of-the-art baseline alternatives across all the datasets. In particular, BioLORD-STAMB2 significantly outperforms SapBERT on CADEC (58.69 vs 40.42) and SMM4H (46.51 vs 43.37). We also observe that BioLORD-STAMB2, the general-domain model, outperforms BioLORD-PMB, the domain-specific variant, proving that the findings of the original BioLORD paper extend to the social media domain.

Our results also highlight that the newly-introduced BioLORD-STAMB2-STS2 manages to move the needle even further (with an average accuracy gain of 1 point with respect to BioLORD-STAMB2), indicating that priming general-purpose models (STAMB2) for biomedical text understanding (STS) before and after the BioLORD pre-training enables to achieve better performance.

On the CADEC dataset in particular, our BioLORD family of models achieves zero-shot accuracy@1 of above 60% for Preferred Term classification. To the best of our knowledge, this is by far the best zero-shot performance ever reported for this dataset.

This seems to confirm that ADE normalization will continue to move towards self-supervised contrastive models, as these models perform well, are very versatile, and can be used to map concepts to any new updated ontology at test time without requiring any retraining. In a field where such models are expected to continue to thrive, the improvements proposed in this paper should be particularly of interest to other researchers.

5 Conclusion

In this paper, we confirmed that BioLORD is an effective pre-training strategy for biomedical entity normalization. We were additionally able to show that applying BioLORD on general-purpose models like STAMB2 provides additional benefits, and that these benefits are more important for sources originating from social media than from clinical notes. Finally, we report that STS-fine-tuning of models both before and after undergoing the BioLORD pre-training can bring additional benefits even in the ADE normalization task, especially in the case when the source originates from social media documents.

Limitations

This paper did not investigate the impact of the proposed pre-training strategies on ADE identification, the task of finding ADE mentions in a text.

We also did not investigate the impact of fine-tuning models on the task, although we have performed some preliminary experiments on this, which seem to confirm the conclusions for zero-shot models apply to fine-tuned models as well.

Ethics Statement

The authors do not foresee that their work would raised any particular ethical concern.

References

Ebtsam Adel, Shaker El-Sappagh, Sherif Barakat, and Mohammed Elmogy. 2019. Chapter 13 - ontology-based electronic health record semantic interoperability: A survey. In Nilanjan Dey, Amira S. Ashour, Simon James Fong, and Surekha Borra, editors, *U-Healthcare Monitoring Systems*, Advances in Ubiquitous Sensing Applications for Healthcare, pages 315–352. Academic Press.

Nestor Alvaro, Yusuke Miyao, and Nigel Collier. 2017. TwiMed: Twitter and PubMed comparable corpus of drugs, diseases, symptoms, and their relations. *JMIR Public Health Surveill.*, 3(2):e24.

Bissan Audeh, Florelle Bellet, Marie-Noëlle Beyens, Agnès Lillo-Le Louët, and Cédric Bousquet. 2020. Use of social media for pharmacovigilance activities: Key findings and recommendations from the Vigi4Med project. *Drug Saf.*, 43(9):835–851.

Olivier Bodenreider. 2004. The Unified Medical Language System (UMLS): Integrating Biomedical Terminology. *Nucleic Acids Research*, 32:D267–70.

Elliot G Brown, Louise Wood, and Sue Wood. 1999. The Medical Dictionary for Regulatory Activities (MedDRA). *Drug Safety*, 20(2):109–117.

Ting Chen, Simon Kornblith, Mohammad Norouzi, and Geoffrey Hinton. 2020. A simple framework for contrastive learning of visual representations. *arXiv preprint arXiv:2002.05709*.

Leo Gao, Stella Biderman, Sid Black, Laurence Golding, Travis Hoppe, Charles Foster, Jason Phang, Horace He, Anish Thite, Noa Nabeshima, Shawn Presser, and Connor Leahy. 2020. The pile: An 800gb dataset of diverse text for language modeling.

Graciela Gonzalez-Hernandez, Ari Z. Klein, Ivan Flores, Davy Weissenbacher, Arjun Magge, Karen O'Connor, Abeed Sarker, Anne-Lyse Minard, Elena Tutubalina, Zulfat Miftahutdinov, and Ilseyar Alimova, editors. 2020. *Proceedings of the Fifth Social Media Mining for Health Applications Workshop & Shared Task*. Association for Computational Linguistics, Barcelona, Spain (Online).

Yu Gu, Robert Tinn, Hao Cheng, Michael Lucas, Naoto Usuyama, Xiaodong Liu, Tristan Naumann, Jianfeng Gao, and Hoifung Poon. 2020. Domain-specific language model pretraining for biomedical natural language processing.

International Health Terminology Standards Development Organisation IHTSDO. 2008. Snomed: Clinical terms. `https://www.snomed.org/`. Accessed: 2023-04-27.

Alistair E.W. Johnson, Tom J. Pollard, Lu Shen, Liwei H. Lehman, Mengling Feng, Mohammad Ghassemi, Benjamin Moody, Peter Szolovits, Leo Anthony Celi, and Roger G. Mark. 2016. Mimic-iii, a freely accessible critical care database. *Scientific Data*, 3(1):160035.

Sarvnaz Karimi, Alejandro Metke-Jimenez, Madonna Kemp, and Chen Wang. 2015. Cadec: A corpus of adverse drug event annotations. *Journal of Biomedical Informatics*, 55:73–81.

Fangyu Liu, Ehsan Shareghi, Zaiqiao Meng, Marco Basaldella, and Nigel Collier. 2021. Self-alignment pretraining for biomedical entity representations. In *Proceedings of the 2021 Conference of the North American Chapter of the Association for Computational Linguistics: Human Language Technologies*, pages 4228–4238, Online. Association for Computational Linguistics.

Dimitra Pappa and Lampros K. Stergioulas. 2019. Harnessing social media data for pharmacovigilance: a review of current state of the art, challenges and future directions. *International Journal of Data Science and Analytics*, 8(2):113–135.

Beatrice Portelli, Simone Scaboro, Enrico Santus, Hooman Sedghamiz, Emmanuele Chersoni, and Giuseppe Serra. 2022. Generalizing over long tail concepts for medical term normalization. In *Proceedings of the 2022 Conference on Empirical Methods in Natural Language Processing*, pages 8580–8591, Abu Dhabi, United Arab Emirates. Association for Computational Linguistics.

Nils Reimers and Iryna Gurevych. 2019. Sentence-bert: Sentence embeddings using siamese bert-networks. In *Proceedings of the 2019 Conference on Empirical Methods in Natural Language Processing*. Association for Computational Linguistics.

François Remy, Kris Demuynck, and Thomas Demeester. 2022. BioLORD: Learning ontological representations from definitions for biomedical concepts and their textual descriptions. In *Findings of the Association for Computational Linguistics: EMNLP 2022*, pages 1454–1465, Abu Dhabi, United Arab Emirates. Association for Computational Linguistics.

Eric W Sayers, Jeffrey Beck, Evan E Bolton, Devon Bourexis, James R Brister, Kathi Canese, Donald C Comeau, Kathryn Funk, Sunghwan Kim, William Klimke, Aron Marchler-Bauer, Melissa Landrum, Stacy Lathrop, Zhiyong Lu, Thomas L Madden, Nuala O'Leary, Lon Phan, Sanjida H Rangwala, Valerie A Schneider, Yuri Skripchenko, Jiyao Wang, Jian Ye, Barton W Trawick, Kim D Pruitt, and Stephen T Sherry. 2021. Database resources of the national center for biotechnology information. *Nucleic Acids Res.*, 49(D1):D10–D17.

Mujeen Sung, Hwisang Jeon, Jinhyuk Lee, and Jaewoo Kang. 2020. Biomedical entity representations with synonym marginalization. In *Proceedings of the 58th Annual Meeting of the Association for Computational Linguistics*, pages 3641–3650, Online. Association for Computational Linguistics.

Yanshan Wang, Naveed Afzal, Sunyang Fu, Liwei Wang, Feichen Shen, Majid Rastegar-Mojarad, and

Hongfang Liu. 2020. Medsts: a resource for clinical semantic textual similarity. *Language Resources and Evaluation*, 54(1):57–72.

Davy Weissenbacher, Abeed Sarker, Arjun Magge, Ashlynn Daughton, Karen O'Connor, Michael J. Paul, and Graciela Gonzalez-Hernandez. 2019. Overview of the fourth social media mining for health (SMM4H) shared tasks at ACL 2019. In *Proceedings of the Fourth Social Media Mining for Health Applications (#SMM4H) Workshop & Shared Task*, pages 21–30, Florence, Italy. Association for Computational Linguistics.

Zheng Yuan, Zhengyun Zhao, Haixia Sun, Jiao Li, Fei Wang, and Sheng Yu. 2022. Coder: Knowledge-infused cross-lingual medical term embedding for term normalization. *Journal of Biomedical Informatics*, 126:103983.

Maryam Zolnoori, Kin Wah Fung, Timothy B. Patrick, Paul Fontelo, Hadi Kharrazi, Anthony Faiola, Nilay D. Shah, Yi Shuan Shirley Wu, Christina E. Eldredge, Jake Luo, Mike Conway, Jiaxi Zhu, Soo Kyung Park, Kelly Xu, and Hamideh Moayyed. 2019. The psytar dataset: From patients generated narratives to a corpus of adverse drug events and effectiveness of psychiatric medications. *Data in Brief*, 24:103838.